Serious Games: Games That Educate, Train, and Inform

DAVID MICHAEL AND SANDE CHEN

THOMSON

COURSE TECHNOLOGY

Professional ■ Technical ■ Reference

ISBN: 1-59200-622-1

Library of Congress Catalog Card Number: 2005927427

Printed in Canada

06 07 08 09 10 PH 10 9 8 7 6 5 4 3 2

Publisher and General Manager, Thomson Course Technology PTR:
Stacy L. Hiquet

Associate Director of Marketing:
Sarah O'Donnell

Manager of Editorial Services:
Heather Talbot

Marketing Manager:
Jordan Casey

Senior Acquisitions Editor:
Emi Smith

Senior Editor:
Mark Garvey

Project Editor and Copyeditor:
Kim V. Benbow

Thomson Course Technology PTR Editorial Services Coordinator:
Elizabeth Furbish

Interior Layout Tech:
Shawn Morningstar

Cover Designer:
Charlie Allensworth
and Mike Tanamachi

Indexer:
Kelly Talbot

Proofreader:
Sara Gullion

Thomson Course Technology PTR, a division of Thomson Course Technology
25 Thomson Place
Boston, MA 02210
http://www.courseptr.com

*For Mom & Dad—thanks for all the encouragement
and support you've given me over the years.
I wouldn't be here if you hadn't been there.*

—DRM

For my parents—thank you for your love and support.

—SC

FOREWORD

Games have power. Games have the power to teach, to train, to educate. Games have the power to bring people together—young, old, and in between. Games have the power to reveal and build character. Games have the power to retain and promote health. Games have the power to heal. On the other side of the force, gambling games have the power to enrich or to bankrupt.

This applies to games inclusively, encompassing not only video games and computer games but also non-digital forms of codified play, engaged in by people alone or in groups.

In preschool and in kindergarten, children are taught games as a socializing activity and to prepare children for organized learning. Who among us has not played Musical Chairs, Duck Duck Goose, Hide and Seek, Mother May I, Simon Says, or Capture the Flag? Some of these games we learned from our peers, or at camp, or at birthday parties. Others were introduced to us by our teachers.

In *The Republic*, Plato drew the connection between play and education; he recommended the use of games for the education of children. And for young adult students, he saw philosophical discourse—wordplay, to stretch the point—as an educational game. Plato developed the notion of hypothetical questions (thought experiments, or philosophical games) as a way to examine opposing philosophical viewpoints. Such mental play imparted Plato's students with the ability to see both sides of an issue so that they could govern well and fairly.

Military officers have used games like Chaturanga, Chess, Go (Wei Qi, Baduk), and Xiang Qi (Chinese Chess) to teach important concepts of strategy and tactics for over a thousand years.

Games bring people together. Girls have long socialized by means of rhyming jump rope games and Hopscotch. Boys get together to play physical sports games and collectible card games such as *Pokémon* and *Yu-Gi-Oh*. As we grow a little older, other games like Telephone (also known as Chinese Whispers or Whisper Down The Lane) not only increase our socialization skills but even teach us about the complexities of communication and human psychology. Men socialize over Poker; women enjoy getting together for good times and snacks over a rousing game of Bunco, Pan, or Canasta. Families enjoy quality time with *Yahtzee*, Rummy, *Clue*, and *Monopoly*, and shout answers at the TV during *Jeopardy!* and *Wheel of Fortune*. Couples socialize over games such as Backgammon, *Trivial Pursuit*, *Uno*, *Scrabble*, and charades.

It was Plato, again, who said, "You can discover more about a person in an hour of play than in a year of conversation." You can learn volumes about a person's character in an hour of playing games, whether it's Bridge, Poker, *Magic: The Gathering*, or even (perhaps especially) *Grand Theft Auto*.

Electronic educational games for young children take up whole aisles of shelf space in our toy stores. In the twilight of our lives, games like Bingo, Bridge, and Mah-Jongg not only provide social connectivity but also exercise our gray cells. When not socializing, there are solitary games like *Solitaire*, *FreeCell*, and crosswords to keep our brains sharp and alive.

Simple card puzzle games like Concentration, or computerized tile-matching games like *Shanghai*, are used as therapy for patients suffering from learning disorders or brain injuries. Such games help teach important skills like short-term memory retention, pattern recognition, category sorting, and of course hand-eye coordination.

But as with any force, there is not only a list of ways it can be used for good. Games can have a dark side as well. Many marriages have ended in divorce over addictions to gambling games or even MMORPGs, like *Everquest*.

The above are examples of the likely unintended side effects of games that were undoubtedly designed primarily to entertain. The purpose of this book is to aid designers in building beneficial effects into their games by design rather than by accident or serendipity. An understanding of the mechanics of what makes a good game, and how games can achieve these "serious" goals, can help us in our quest to make games that do more than merely entertain.

We as game designers understand the power of what we do, perhaps without having thought much about it. That power may well be an unconscious motivation driving us into the profession. But whether we strive to create games to entertain, or games to teach or train, we love our work. For game designers, designing games is one of the best games around.

"We always hear 'Life is short, play hard.' But what about 'Life is short, work hard'?"

—Dean Kamen (inventor of the Segway Personal Transporter)

"Work and play are words used to describe the same thing under differing conditions."

—Mark Twain

—Tom Sloper, www.sloperama.com

BIO

Tom Sloper designed his first board game in 1977, and started designing games professionally a few years later, creating LCD games for watches and calculators (*Game Time*, *Arcade Time*, *Chase-N-Counter*, *Space-N-Counter*) before moving on to video game consoles like the Vectrex and the Atari 2600. He worked as a designer and producer at Western Technologies, Sega Enterprises, Atari Corporation, and Activision. When not competing in international Mah-Jongg competitions, he writes, teaches, and consults, doing business as Sloperama Productions.

ACKNOWLEDGMENTS

The authors would like to thank all those who took the time to talk to us about serious games: Phineas Barnes, Ian Bogost, Russell Bowers, Jim Brazell, Asaf Burak, Col. Matt Caffrey, Randy Chase, Van Collins, Brody Condon, Kevin Corti, Lauren Davis, Tim Emmerich, Jonathan Ferguson, Craig Fryar, Aaron Greb, Eric Keylor, Eric Klopfer, Joan Leandre, Greg LoPiccolo, Eric Marcoullier, Mike McShaffry, Marc Prensky, Clark Quinn, Kent Quirk, Jason Robar, Ben Sawyer, Tim Sweeney, Deborah Tillett, Judy Tryer, Col. Casey Wardynski, Carey Wargo, and Dr. Mark Wiederhold. We would also like to thank our editors Emi Smith and Kim Benbow, Dave Astle and GameDev.net, Bernard Beam, Imelda Kataraharajan, Charlie Allensworth, Tom Sloper, and Chris Oltyan for their help, as well as everyone who completed our Serious Games Survey. And, of course, Sonata.

ABOUT THE AUTHORS

David "RM" Michael has been a successful independent software developer for over 10 years, working in a variety of industries, including video games. He is the owner of DavidRM Software (www.davidrm.com) and co-owner of Samu Games (www.samugames.com). Michael is the author of *The Indie Game Development Survival Guide*, and his articles about game design, development, and the game development industry have appeared on GameDev.net (www.gamedev.net) and in the book *Game Design Perspectives*. His blog about independent games, serious games, and independent software is Joe Indie (www.joeindie.com).

Sande Chen has been active in the gaming industry for over five years. She has written for mainstream and industry publications, including *Secrets of the Game Business*, and was a speaker at the 2005 Game Developers Conference. Her past game credits include Independent Games Festival winner *Terminus*, *Scooby-Doo*, and *JamDat Scrabble*. Chen holds dual degrees in economics and in writing and humanistic studies from the Massachusetts Institute of Technology, an M.Sc. in economics from the London School of Economics, and an M.F.A. in cinema-television from the University of Southern California. In 1996, she was nominated for a Grammy in music video direction. She currently works as a freelance writer/game designer.

CONTENTS

INTRODUCTION

With the success and proliferation of video games, there can be no doubt that video games are a part of our culture as much as books, movies, television, and other forms of media. In fact, video games often serve as the inspiration for books and movies instead of the other way around. And just like books, movies, and television, video games have the potential to be more than just entertainment.

Government agencies, the military, hospitals, non-profit organizations, corporations, and schools at every educational level now use video games as a part of training or education. The goal of *Serious Games: Games That Educate, Train, and Inform* is to help game developers learn how to take what they've learned from making games for entertainment purposes and apply those techniques to making "serious games": games for education, training, healing, and more.

More Than "Edutainment"

Serious games are more than just "edutainment," that 1990s-era attempt to cash in on the growth of the multi-media PC market and the increasing prevalence of computers in schools. Serious games encompass the same goals of edutainment, but extend far past teaching facts and rote memorization to include all aspects of education: teaching, training, and informing.

Education through entertainment was the goal of edutainment, but it was targeted primarily at preschool and young children. Focused on reading, math, and science, edutainment titles were often hosted by cute animals or licensed children's television characters to provide the "entertainment." However, not all students are under the age of 10, and there are plenty of other subjects that can be explored using much more compelling methods.

Advances in computer hardware and software allow games to move into other aspects of education or training. Many skills can be taught only by *doing*, and many lessons can be learned only through failure. Serious games allow training to occur in a non-lethal environment. Routinely, soldiers enter complex, highly detailed simulations with 3D rendering and real-world physics calculations to practice their military training. Similarly, mental health patients, when presented with a game to help deal with their treatment, feel an environment of safety.

Finally, not all teaching involves facts and practice. Serious games can be used to inform their players of environmental issues, health issues, political views, and more. As an expressive art form, games already present a point of view, though often unintentionally or only as a consequence of the game's content or storyline. There is no reason why a game couldn't be designed with the express intent of conveying a particular viewpoint, whether it be political, personal, emotional, or any other aspect of human existence.

All of these possibilities of serious games will be explored.

A New Opportunity

Serious games represent a fast-emerging opportunity that will give game developers a chance to gain a share of the rapidly expanding revenue pie for educational tools. Spending on educational tools is at an all-time high, with money coming from both public and private sources. According to Ben Sawyer, co-founder of the Serious Games Initiative, the market for serious games today is at $20 million and is expected to grow over the next decade. Consider the following: In 2003, the global education and training market was estimated at $2 trillion. Technology research firm IDC predicts that by 2008, 40 percent of U.S. companies will adopt serious games in their training efforts. Already, the U.S. Army spends nearly $7 billion annually on training, and other government agencies are following the Army's lead. Health organizations and other groups are only just beginning to realize the powerful reach of games.

More than just a new revenue stream, though, serious games offer a new wellspring of ideas and techniques that can help entertainment-oriented games have more meaning, deliver a richer experience, and even develop as an expressive art form.

When educators attempt to make games on their own, or game developers attempt to create educational material, the result is often similar to the worst edutainment has to offer: trite, ineffectual gameplay presenting minimal information outside of a single context. Imagine the possibilities if the two groups came together, each bringing their excitement and dedication to the different aspects of their projects.

INTENDED AUDIENCE

This book is primarily intended for game developers, both industry and independent, who

- Want to learn more about serious games and the growing market they represent.

- Are looking for alternatives to the traditional publisher-funded revenue model.

- Need projects to keep production teams busy between retail projects.

- Want to extend the video game medium even further into the mass culture.

In addition, serious game purchasers and customers—trainers and educators in public, private, and military sectors—will find this book a valuable introduction to the potential of this popular new medium that is computer games. Case studies of how professionals in various markets utilize games will give not only ideas and inspiration but also credibility. This may be especially important when seeking approval for game-related projects.

IN THIS BOOK

Serious Games: Games That Educate, Train, and Inform begins in Part 1 with an overview of serious games and presents the opportunity represented by serious games for the game developer as well as for the various industries and markets that will be covered in the upcoming chapters.

Part 2 of the book provides detailed information about each of the major markets for serious games: the military, educators, government agencies, corporations, hospitals, non-profit organizations, religious groups, and activist groups. The description of each market will include a brief history of what has been done with video games in those markets, what is happening today, what is anticipated in the future, and more:

- Goals of each emerging market
- Types of games of interest to the market
- Market-specific issues for developers to consider

Finally, in Appendix A, you will find a list of some of the new and existing conferences and organizations that have grown up around serious games. Some of these are new, having met only once or twice as of this publication, but others have been around for decades. Appendix B includes the results of a serious games survey conducted by the authors.

Game developers have tended to ignore and/or not take seriously the educational benefits of their games, while educators have often considered games a distraction or worse—a source of educational problems. This book attempts to introduce each group to the other and show them what they can accomplish if they work together.

Part

1

What Are Serious Games?

Part 1 of *Serious Games: Games That Educate, Train, and Inform* introduces the specific issues surrounding serious games. While many of the techniques and processes used may be similar to those of entertainment games, there are certain differences.

Chapter 1, "New Opportunities for Game Developers," provides an overview of the opportunity represented by serious games—for game developers as well as for the various industries and markets that will be covered in the next part of the book. For game developers, serious games can offer new markets and new revenue streams, and even a new path into the industry. For educators in all industries, serious games provide a powerful, possibly revolutionary, new training tool.

Chapter 2, "Serious Games Defined," offers a comprehensive definition of serious games and shows how even education and learning have their basis in games and play. Video games are maturing as a medium and with that maturity comes the opportunity and the responsibility to do more than just entertain.

Chapter 3, "Serious Games Design and Development Issues," closes Part 1 by covering design issues specific to serious games. Games for entertainment focus on gameplay and providing the most fun to the player. Serious games, however, must be concerned with the accuracy of what they simulate and present to the player. Fun isn't eliminated, of course, but it is no longer the primary thrust of the design. Training or education becomes the main goal.

New Opportunities for Game Developers

Three of the biggest challenges faced by independent game developers (that is, those not owned by a publisher) are the development of new technology, the creation of content required for ever-bigger games, and the task of keeping their development teams busy between projects.

The retail video game industry has historically been driven by technology. Whether it's new hardware or new software, developers have been chasing a moving target. This moving target can make it hard for developers to see a return on investment in technology because they have to discard what they've done and recreate it for the next generation of hardware, software, and customer expectations.

While there have been some stabilizing influences in the technology used by video games, the content required for video games continues to grow. The team of artists, modelers, and musicians working on AAA retail titles has grown to be two, three, five, and even 10 times the size of the programming team. Since the content created is usually tied to the technology in a particular game, much of it is not useful on future projects.

This growth of the teams needed to build video games makes employee costs the single largest budget item of game projects. Meeting payroll for these large teams, especially after the project has ended and no milestone payments are coming in can be a serious challenge. This challenge has proven to be the end of many independent game developers.

This chapter shows how serious games can help developers realize a greater return on their investment in technology and content while avoiding or reducing the impact of downtime between retail projects. Furthermore, serious games may allow developers to enter other markets beyond retail outlets, increasing the possibility of multiple revenue streams. Finally, serious games can allow developers to experiment with new styles of gameplay and even new distribution avenues.

Serious games are not all good news and gravy train, though, and this chapter also talks about the new challenges that come with the new opportunities. Learning how to deal with public sources of funding is just one of the complicated issues that most game developers may not have faced before.

SERIOUS GAMES CAN REDUCE RISK BY USING EXISTING TECHNOLOGY AND CONTENT

Whether developers build their own game engine or license and modify an engine like Criterion's RenderWare, that investment in time and resources is one of the biggest outlays the developer will face. Often only content creation is a greater budget item.

The most obvious way to recoup the investment is to create another game that leverages the engine. Ideally, this new game will not require new technology or significant additions. Content creation will benefit from a tried-and-tested pipeline. If existing content resources can be used again, that's even better.

The retail game market, however, doesn't always offer the best way to leverage existing resources. The long development cycle dictates that the target platform, whether console or personal computer, no longer represents the coveted high end. Plus, with the amount of content required in a retail title growing at a rapid rate, the time dedicated to create the new title becomes considerable.

Serious games, with a few exceptions, do not demand the same level of technological "wow" factor nor the same staggering amount of content.

Military-grade simulations still squeeze all the juice they can out of top-of-the-line hardware and software, but most other categories of serious games can be satisfied with much less. Accuracy of the simulation *behind* the graphics is often the primary goal. Therefore, the prettiest graphics aren't always required.

Thus serious games can be built with smaller teams, using existing technology with proven content pipelines. This in turn allows for much shorter development cycles. Shorter development cycles mean that more products can be completed by the same team. In a survey conducted for this book (see survey result 1.1), game developers, sponsors, and researchers noted the smaller team sizes and shorter development timeframes.

Serious Games Survey Result 1.1

Question: What is/was the team size of your most recent serious games project?

73.77%	1–10
18.03%	11–25
6.56%	26–50
1.64%	51–100

(Survey Note: 61 Respondents)

Question: What is/was the (projected) time frame of your most recent serious games project?

28.33%	1–6 months
35.00%	6 months–1 year
21.67%	1–2 years
13.33%	3–5 years
1.67%	5+ years

(Survey Note: 60 Respondents)

Once they have completed their retail product, game developers could create an internal team whose sole purpose is to seek out ways to re-use what was created for the retail product. This team would research the local government, healthcare, education, and corporate institutions that might be interested in utilizing the accumulated assets. Since this requires control of the intellectual property (IP), such as the source code and art assets, and the ability to have team members that aren't working on the current retail project (non-exclusivity), the developer would need to have this plan in mind before signing the publisher's contract.

Serious games, especially training games, usually target very specific market segments. However, several such games could be created for different market segments, using many of the same technology and content components. Many companies follow this strategy. As indicated by survey result 1.2, serious game developers, sponsors, and researchers noted that there were many possible audiences for their products.

BreakAway Games, a leading serious games developer, has an underwater diving simulator game called *Crate* that is used for training purposes by the United States Navy, but it is also used to relieve the pain of children undergoing chemotherapy. In this case, the exact same game is being used in two very different niches for two very different purposes.

Beyond personal computers in the home and office, serious games are also appearing on consoles like the Sony PlayStation 2 and Microsoft Xbox. Though many serious games do not have the kind of mass market appeal required for console games, the success of new peripherals, such as the EyeToy, and the growth of dance pad games like *Dance Dance Revolution* have fueled an interest in serious games for consoles. As serious games increase in popularity, it's likely that more will appear on the same platforms as retail game products.

Serious Games Survey Result 1.2

Question: *Who has been the target audience(s) of your serious games projects?*

53.97%	Students (any level)
47.62%	General public
26.98%	Corporate management and/or executives
23.40%	Education professionals
23.81%	Government personnel
23.81%	Healthcare professionals
22.22%	Corporate employees
17.46%	Military personnel
7.94%	Healthcare patients (including Mental Health)
7.94%	Emergency Medical Personnel/First Responders
1.59%	Activists
4.76%	Other

(Survey Note: 63 Respondents)

SERIOUS GAMES CAN KEEP TEAMS BUSY BETWEEN RETAIL PROJECTS

New game development shops are often born in the crucible of development of a retail title for a publisher, only to die in the long, dry period between the end of one project and the beginning of another.

The development team is put together as the project grows, using funds acquired from the publisher as milestones are reached. Once the project is completed, though, and the final advance check cashed, developers are faced with an extended period of time in which they have a lot of employees expecting paychecks—and no income. Even if the company managed to save some of their advance, the "burn rate" for even just 20 employees can exceed $100,000 per month. And that's a small team by modern standards. Imagine the burn rate of a team of 50, or even 100, employees.

So what happens? Sometimes, the shop lands a new publisher-funded contract quickly. More often, however, is that the months stretch out, either because the developer can't find a publisher who is interested in the next idea or because contract negotiations occur at the glacial speed of business. The shop begins to let people go, hoping to hire them again when the deal is ready. Sometimes the deal goes through. Sometimes it doesn't. A lot of game development shops don't survive this kind of inter-project stress.

Serious games may be able to offer an alternative. With their reduced technology requirements, smaller content footprint, and quicker turnaround, serious game projects may be a perfect fit for the time between big retail contracts.

When asked in a survey (see survey result 1.3) whether or not serious game development was compatible with entertainment game development, serious game developers indicated that it was quite synergistic to do both types of development.

While serious games don't always have the same kind of budgets as AAA retail games, they are still worthwhile endeavors. The budgets for serious games can range from tens of thousands up to tens of millions. The most common budgets, though, are less than $1 million. The agencies and organizations interested in funding serious games often do not have the same kind of deep pockets as the game publishers. However, in the period between retail projects, when no money is coming in at all, any revenue is likely to be good revenue and could make the difference between laying off a few people and sending home the entire team. It could mean survival as a business or shutting the doors for good.

As shown by survey result 1.4, large budgets for serious games are possible, but most companies land smaller contracts.

Serious Games Survey Result 1.3

Question: If you are a developer, do you only develop serious games?

62.50% No

37.50% Yes

(Survey Note: 56 Respondents)

Question: If not, do you see much overlap between your entertainment and serious game projects?

80.00% Yes

20.00% No

(Survey Note: 37 Respondents)

Serious Games Survey Result 1.4

Question: What is/was the budget of your most recent serious games project?

18.03% $0 – $5000

8.20% $5001 – $10,000

9.84% $10,001 – $50,000

9.84% $50,001 – $100,000

26.23% $100,001 – $500,000

11.48% $500,001 – $1,000,000

14.75% $1,000,001 – $10,000,000

1.64% $10,000,000+

(Survey Note: 61 Respondents)

In conclusion, as described earlier, creating an internal team solely for the purpose of seeking serious game opportunities is one approach to utilizing employees that with the completion of the most recent project have transitioned from "essential" to "extra." It might even be better to create such a team *before* the completion of the retail project so that there is a possibility of a new project ramping up within a couple weeks or months. Again, this kind of pre-emptive action, during-the-project team re-assignment might require special contract negotiations or permission from the publisher.

SERIOUS GAMES CAN EXPERIMENT WITH ALTERNATIVE PLAY STYLES

The small budgets and specific target markets of serious games may offer developers the chance to experiment with totally new styles of gameplay, user interfaces, and game design. With far fewer resources on the line, serious game designers can be more creative. The reduced resources can actually force designers to be more innovative as they struggle to create a game under such constraints.

The subject matter of serious games may include possibilities for new ways to display the game to the player or new ways to get input from the player. Representing and interacting with abstract concepts such as voter attitudes and subatomic particles could open up new possibilities. The subject matter itself might prove to be a whole new source of entertaining gameplay concepts. Subjects for games have tended to be constrained by what has been done before. Japanese games have tended to go further afield, sometimes creating for entertainment what in the U.S. would be thought of as serious games.

The reverse is also true: Using an established game user interface to present real-world information may help serious games buyers with a new way to look at their issues. Game simulations are seldom 100 percent accurate, but they do offer a way to simplify abstract problems in a way that even untrained people can understand them.

SERIOUS GAMES CAN EXPERIMENT WITH ALTERNATIVE DISTRIBUTION

The growth of the Internet in the 1990s opened up the possibility of digital distribution of games. Though the percentage of games sold through digital distribution is still small, it continues to climb every year.

Retail AAA games, with their huge number of art assets creating a huge download package, have been slow to utilize this new distribution channel. The growth of broadband since the dawn of the 21st century has been making it more feasible, however, and growth is accelerating. Serious games, with their smaller budgets, team size, shorter development cycles, and smaller final products provide an opportunity for developers to experiment with selling those games direct to players, broadband optional.

At first glance, many serious games appear so specific in their target market that finding players outside of that niche seems unlikely. By simply offering the game via the Web, developers may discover that a whole new market has been waiting for them.

While the money from direct sales to consumers and players may not start out as much, it's still revenue. Such games may also help the developer reduce its dependence on the retail publishers. For smaller developers, any additional cashflow can be helpful. Moreover, these games may attract the attention of retail publishers looking to expand into the serious games space.

On the other hand, "vertical" products, products that service a particular industry or market segment, have been very profitable. These vertical markets are the domain of highly profitable corporations and businesses, which allow for much higher price points and much richer profit margins because the products are tailored to the specific needs of the market. A product that supports one vertical market can often be retooled to serve the needs of a similar vertical market. This is the approach used by Cyberlore, an independent game developer who is leveraging the social simulation engine of their game, *Playboy: The Mansion*, to create training software for a large corporation. Cyberlore is the subject of a case study in Chapter 7, "Corporate Games."

So with serious games, a developer could experiment with distribution that bypasses the retail publishers and has the potential to open up new business models and revenue streams.

SERIOUS GAMES CAN OPEN UP NEW FUNDING POSSIBILITIES

Along with new distribution, serious games offer access to additional sources of funding. Traditionally, the retail video game publishers have been the primary source of funding for video games. Serious games, however, are of interest to a much wider collection of organizations, foundations, and individuals.

The government, especially the military, is the largest source of funds for serious games. The government has programs like the Small Business Innovation Research (SBIR), which we will cover in detail later. There are quite a few other groups that have money to spend on serious games. Among them are the following:

- Public and private foundations

- Non-government organizations (NGOs)

- Universities

- Corporations, including retail chains

- Non-profit organizations

- Individuals

- Other governments

- Publishers

We will cover all of these groups in Part 2 of this book.

Serious Games Can Make You Part of Your Community

To move beyond simple profit motive, serious games also give developers a chance to give back to their communities. Game developers are part of the larger community that surrounds them. And there's much more going on in those communities than game development.

Every community, big or small, has a rich history and goals for the future. Both of these, past and future, as well as the present, are excellent material for serious games. Such games can teach local school students about the community's colorful history. They can help community officials to communicate and decide policy issues, or they can show the impact or benefit of plans for expansion.

Are the city fathers planning another "cosmetic dam" on the river that runs through downtown? Do they want to build a new event arena or other construction to be funded with a new sales tax? Even if you don't have a definite opinion on these issues, someone does, and he or she may be willing to fund a quick (a key word in local politics) game or simulation that demonstrates the negative or positive effects of the proposal. The attention such a game brings, especially from the local press, could help you grow your business.

The point is that these groups exist and they may be looking for a game developer in the local area who is willing to take on the project. The problem they face, though, is that they don't really know where to look or who to ask. So you could become the solution to someone's problem.

These local-interest games may seem to have a very limited market, but with the power of the Internet, their reach could be much greater than originally thought. "All politics is local," Tip O'Neill said, but an issue in one city or region is often an issue in many others. Your local issue game may be able to be used elsewhere in your nation or even internationally.

Also, many cities in the United States have international "sister cities," located on other continents (see Sister Cities International at www.sister-cities.org).

The goal of Sister Cities International is to "promote peace through mutual respect, understanding, and cooperation—one individual, one community at a time." Games that describe your city, show the local culture, or just give a feel for what it's like to live in that city can be a new kind of "international ambassador of good will."

Beyond the local community, there is also the county or parish, the state, and even the nation. All of these are communities that game developers can join. The opportunities for participating in and contributing to these communities are almost endless.

The above represents just a few ideas for how game developers can use serious games to give back to their local community or region. It's also possible to use serious games to help bolster the reputation of the video game industry to the larger national and world communities. Most of the media attention for video games has tended to be negative. Game developers who create games that teach valuable skills, that bring awareness to political and social issues, and that help make the world a better place overall could do a lot to help improve the global opinion of the video game industry as a whole.

On the Other Hand

Serious games are not all new markets and new revenue, however. There are new processes to learn—especially in regards to procuring funding—and new challenges to face.

Serious games are a very different market than traditional retail, with different expectations, budgets, and profit margins. It can be difficult for developers to attract and maintain both markets at the same time. This divided focus can be distracting. Also, as business on one side of the divide grows, there will be increased competition for resources and attention.

Experienced developers may not think there's anything more painful than the process of pitching a game to a publisher and the ensuing negotiations over content, storyline, and milestones. In the serious games arena, though, imagine the same process with clients who are even more finicky, less sure of what it is they want and are trying to achieve, and (often) have less money to offer. If you think it's hard to convince a publisher to fully fund your $5 million dollar project, imagine explaining to a corporate financial officer from a health insurance company how he's going to get that large sum back in training or safety savings.

Currently, the budgets for serious games are much smaller, outside the military and corporate arenas especially, with thinner profit margins. And royalties are virtually non-existent. Most serious games are "work for hire" products with no back end money. Developers work as contractors in most cases.

The design of serious games also diverges from the design of games intended for retail. These design issues are discussed in Chapter 3, "Serious Games Design and Development Issues."

These issues do not mean that it is impossible to mix both traditional game development and serious games development. It only means that serious games need to be approached and handled with an understanding and appreciation of their particular nature.

BreakAway Games is an example of a company that has made serious games a part of their business plan. They create original games for retail and also do serious games for the military and other government agencies. They make it work by leveraging pre-existing art and code assets, when they can, to cross-collateralize effort and expense over multiple projects. A number of smaller, independent game developers already mix "work for hire" contracts with game development in a similar manner. So the mix of business approaches can work well together.

Though there may be few, if any, royalties from serious games, in many cases the developer owns and controls the bulk of the intellectual property of the resulting game. This allows the developer to generate additional revenue by creating updates or selling similar, customized games to other companies and organizations.

CONCLUSION

Serious games offer developers ways to reduce, cross-collateralize, or otherwise mitigate some of the costs of developing technology and content for games. Serious games can also help developers keep their teams busy between larger, retail-oriented projects. In addition, serious games can allow the developer chances to experiment with new styles of gameplay and even new types of distribution.

There are, of course, challenges to working in both the retail and serious games arenas. The two markets can be very different as the sources of funding and the motives for development bear few similarities. It is not impossible to operate successfully in both, however, and the two types of game could prove complementary to each other.

In the next chapter we discuss in detail what exactly are serious games.

SERIOUS GAMES DEFINED

What is a "serious game"?

Ask most game developers and hardcore game players about "serious games" and you will learn that *all* games are serious. In other words, developers and players take their games very seriously. They live to make games, and they live to play games. What could be more serious than that?

To the population at large, however, the term "serious games" sounds like an oxymoron. The two words seem mutually exclusive. How can something be both serious and a game?

So, again, what is a serious game?

A simple explanation that many professionals use in this field, with some reservations and qualifications, is: *A serious game is a game in which education (in its various forms) is the primary goal, rather than entertainment.*

This definition helps clear up the seeming oxymoron, but it no doubt also raises the hackles of people (both game developers and educators) who see entertainment and education as being at odds. It is the contention of this book, however, that not only are education and entertainment *not* in conflict, but that there are many places where the two overlap and where each side can use the tools of the other to achieve their goals.

To that end, in this chapter we will talk about games and the importance of games and play to human culture and activities—including education and learning—and why game designers are in a unique position to help educators.

What Is a Game?

Everyone knows what games are. They've been playing games since they were children. This universal experience, though, and the broad scope of all possible games, makes it difficult to have a single definition of the word "game" that everyone agrees on. To some, games require competition, one or more players, or teams striving to "win." But what about games played alone, with no direct competition? In his book, *Serious Games*, Clark Abt presented a similar definition, but he also talked about the limitations of that definition:

> *Reduced to its formal essence, a game is an activity among two or more independent decision-makers seeking to achieve their objectives in some limiting context. A more conventional definition would say that a game is a context with rules among adversaries trying to win objectives.*

> *The trouble with this definition is that not all games are contests among adversaries—in some games the players cooperate to achieve a common goal against an obstructing force or natural situation that is itself not really a player because it does not have objectives.*

To others, games require rules. To still others, rules are anathema to fun. The philosopher Bernard Suits, in his book, *Grasshopper: Games, Life and Utopia*, had this to say about rules in games:

> *To play a game is to engage in activity directed towards bringing about a specific state of affairs, using only means permitted by rules, where the rules prohibit more efficient in favor of less efficient means, and where such rules are accepted just because they make possible such activity.*

Yet all these definitions about competition and rules seem to suggest that fun and play have little to do with games. Popular opinion would surely disagree. But is there a difference between play and games? Are all games a form of play, or is play part of a game?

The dictionary is no help in this debate. The Webster's Ninth New Collegiate Dictionary from Merriam-Webster lists four broad definitions of "game" (play, tactic, competition, and animals), each with two or three subdefinitions. It seems that games are another of those nebulous concepts that we know when we see but have a hard time defining.

Johan Huizinga, in his 1950 book *Homo Ludens*, provides a definition of "play" that seems equally applicable to "game." He described six characteristics of play:

1. Voluntary, a form of freedom: "play to order is no longer play."

2. Pretend: "play is not 'ordinary' or 'real' life."

3. Immersive, or taking up the player's full attention.

4. "It is 'played out' within certain limits of time and place."

5. Based on rules: "it creates order, *is* order."

6. Social, creating a social group of the players or tending to cause people involved in a particular kind of play to identify themselves as a group.

These six characteristics also seem to describe most games, whether they are card games, board games, party games, or video games. Though he does not explicitly refer to them as such, games might be what Huizinga called a "higher form" of play, described as "a contest *for* something or a representation *of* something."

In summary, games are a voluntary activity, obviously separate from real life, creating an imaginary world that may or may not have any relation to real life and that absorbs the player's full attention. Games are played out within a specific time and place, are played according to established rules, and create social groups out of their players.

WHERE'S THE FUN?

There are some people who will take exception to this definition because it contains no references to "fun." However, "fun" is not an ingredient or something you put in. Fun is a result. In *A Theory of Fun*, Raph Koster defined fun as a side effect of learning something new, something that we "get." The feeling of fun is essentially a positive feedback mechanism to get us to repeat the activity over and over.

A game *can* be fun, but only if the player enjoys playing the game. Since games are a voluntary activity, something the player chooses to do, there is an implication of enjoyment, either in anticipation or based on past experience. In the absence of anticipated enjoyment, or because of an unpleasant earlier experience, the player may choose to not participate or find something else to do. In other words, if a player does not find a game fun, he is unlikely to choose to play it again.

Whether serious games need to be fun, or should be fun, is an ongoing debate. In a survey of serious game developers, educators, and researchers conducted for this book, over 80 percent of respondents felt that the "element of fun" was Important or Very Important (see survey result 2.1).

Serious Games Survey Result 2.1

Question: How do you rate the importance of the "element of fun" in serious games?

33.33%	Very Important
47.62%	Important
15.87%	Useful, but not a primary goal
3.17%	Less Important
0.00%	Not Important

(Survey Note: 63 Respondents)

Serious games often violate one of the six characteristics listed above in that they aren't always voluntary activities. Trainees may indeed be ordered to play a particular game as part of their training. This doesn't mean that the serious game cannot be fun. This is one of the advantages game developers and designers have to offer serious games: the know-how to make something fun. This will be discussed later on in the chapter and in Chapter 3, "Serious Games Design and Development Issues."

Finally, what one person considers a fun simulation may be deadly serious to someone else. For example, the doctor trying to learn the best way to approach an upcoming surgery in a simulation isn't looking to have fun. He or she is trying to save a life by causing the least amount of damage to the affected tissue while still accomplishing the healing objective. In that case, fun must take a backseat to the accuracy of the simulation.

What Is a Serious Game?

With a working definition of games, we can move on to the next question: What is a serious game?

Most games are presented to potential players as an entertaining, enjoyable, and *fun* way to pass the time or interact with other players. But what if the purpose of the game isn't one of these?

Abt described serious games as having an "explicit and carefully thought-out educational purpose":

> *Games may be played seriously or casually. We are concerned*
> *with serious games in the sense that these games have an explicit*
> *and carefully thought-out educational purpose and are not*
> *intended to be played primarily for amusement. This does not*
> *mean that serious games are not, or should not be, entertaining.*

The simplest definition of serious games, then, is games that do not have entertainment, enjoyment, or fun as their primary purpose. That isn't to say that the games under the serious games umbrella *aren't* entertaining, enjoyable, or fun. It's just that there is another purpose, an ulterior motive in a very real sense.

FIGURE 2.1

America's Army

© United States Army. Used with Permission

America's Army (see Figure 2.1), developed by the United States Army as a recruiting tool, when played by a teenager or other civilian can still be an entertaining experience, a chance to "play soldier." Yet the same game and its assets have been repurposed within the Army as a training and testing environment for mission rehearsal, intelligence skills training, first aid and survival training, and more. To an enlisted squad leader preparing for a mission, this game may be an important part of his training. In that instance, whether he finds the game entertaining is not of paramount importance to his superiors. One person's training simulation can be another person's game. For this reason, entertainment games reapplied to other purposes can also be considered serious games.

This tasking of entertainment media to other purposes is not limited to games. Many books throughout the centuries, and movies in the last century, have been written and produced that have similar "serious" messages or intents. John Steinbeck's 1942 novel, *The Moon is Down*, is an example of what could be called a "serious book." Written as a propaganda book and how-to resistance pamphlet for small towns in occupied Europe, it is the story of a small Norwegian town taken over by the Nazis. Despite this ulterior motive, *The Moon is Down* is still a powerful novel in its own right. C. S. Lewis's *Chronicles of Narnia* books are religious allegories, teaching Christian lessons through the fictitious adventures of children and magical creatures. And so on. Most books that have been banned throughout history were blacklisted because they expressed ideas deemed dangerous or seditious by society or the powers that be.

Likewise, in movies, documentaries are the most obvious "serious films." Even mainstream, popular cinema has films that would be considered serious, like *Saving Private Ryan*. *Saving Private Ryan* shows the horror of war at its most personal. In the opening scene, the most powerful in the film, you are there, in an amphibious landing craft, staring down enemy guns, watching people around you die suddenly and brutally, and just hoping you'll survive. Few other films have portrayed the plight of the foot soldier in war so dramatically. Beyond feature films, countless short films have been made, discussing everything from proper grooming habits to sexual harassment sensitivity as well as explaining the hows and whys of such topics as the metric system and customer service call handling.

Some people may argue that this kind of ulterior motive detracts from a game, artistically and in other ways, just as there are people who say such motives detract from books and movies. As an art form, though, all games, from the simplest match-three casual game to the most complex story-driven 3D surround-sound experience, single player or multi-player, have something to say. Art is expression. It's not always profound expression, but it is expression nonetheless.

Thus serious games are games that use the artistic medium of games to deliver a message, teach a lesson, or provide an experience.

Not all serious games cover material *seriously*, however. Ben Sawyer, co-founder of the Serious Games Initiative, has said that the "serious" in "serious games" is intended to reflect the purpose of the game, why it was created, and has no bearing on the content of the game itself.

MORE THAN "JUST EDUTAINMENT"

While the phrase "serious games" is relatively recent, and still new to many people, there is an older term that most will recognize: *edutainment*.

Edutainment, or *education through entertainment*, is a term that came into common use in the 1990s with the appearance of "multi-media" personal computers. Though edutainment is not limited to video games and refers to any form of education that also seeks to entertain, it most often refers to video games with overtly educational aims, specifically for preschoolers and new readers.

Serious games, however, as presented in this book, move past the limited focus of edutainment to encompass all types of education and at all ages. Edutainment titles are considered a subset of the overall topic of serious games.

WHY USE SERIOUS GAMES?

Huizinga saw play as the basis for all culture. Law, philosophy, art, and other aspects of human culture, he contends, arise "in the form of play" and even such serious human activities as war bear the "formal characteristics of play." And, yes, even education. As children we learn to play, and as we grow up, we play to learn, even though sometimes the "play" doesn't *feel* like "play."

Is this really so surprising, though? The traditional schoolroom is centered around teaching the rules for multiplication, economics, history, and so on. Repetition is used to make sure the students remember. While "fun" is often lacking, as is voluntary attendance, the other similarities to play are evident:

- Pretend: school presents the universe in small pieces.
- Immersive: schools' success in teaching requires the attention of the students.
- School happens at a definite time and place.
- School is based on rules.
- School is social, grouping students by age and learning ability.

In the same manner, all games, be they board games, social games, or video games, require the player or players to learn something. At a minimum, the rules of play must be learned. Once the basic rules are mastered, then comes refinement through trying different strategies and ways of applying the rules. Raph Koster gave this list of things that video games already teach:

- Motor skills: hand-eye coordination

- Spatial relationships: 3D and 2D

- Shapes: again, both 3D and 2D

- Curiosity: players learn to test everything, to seek out new information in unexpected places.

In *What Video Games Have to Teach Us About Learning and Literacy*, James Paul Gee wrote

> *Many good computer and video games . . . are long, complex, and difficult, especially for beginners. People are not always eager to do difficult things. Faced with the challenge of getting them to do so, two choices are often available. We can force them, which is the solution schools use. Or, a temptation when profit is at stake, we can dumb down the product. Neither option is open to the game industry, at least for the moment. They can't force people to play, and most avid players don't want their games dumbed down.*

So how do designers get new, inexperienced players to learn how to play their games? Game designers, James Paul Gee said, "have hit on profoundly good methods of getting people to learn and to enjoy learning." In summary, the game designer convinces the player to learn how to play the game by making it fun.

Abt agreed. "Games," he said in his book, "are effective teaching and training devices for students of all ages and in many situations because they are highly motivating, and because they communicate very efficiently the concepts and facts of many subjects." Games give "dramatic representations" of the subject or problem being studied, and allow the players to "assume realistic roles, face problems, formulate strategies, make decisions, and get fast feedback on the consequences of their actions"—all without the cost of real world consequences or errors.

This is the main point of serious games: to get players to learn something, and, if possible, have fun doing it. The new generation of students and trainees has grown up with video games. It's what they're used to. They're more likely to play video games and learn from video games.

Research showing the effectiveness of serious games is beginning to accumulate. A *Wired* article from September 2004 quoted studies showing "that immersion in simulated environments increases learning speed and retention for a range of tasks, from making laparoscopic incisions to rescuing people from burning buildings." A *CBS Evening News* segment in February of 2005 talked about how a video game would keep the player engaged for 2 to 4 hours, while students in a classroom typically lost interest after 15 minutes. Thus serious games could become an important tool in any classroom situation.

WHAT CAN SERIOUS GAMES TEACH?

As we discussed before, all games are a form of expression. Since games express ideas, information, and beliefs, this means that games teach.

Considering the teaching potential of games, what subjects and material are serious games suitable for? Who would be interested in games that teach? The military has used game-like simulations in their training for years. They are not the only ones interested in serious games, however. There are also

- Educators (primary, secondary, and higher)
- Corporations
- Non-government organizations (NGOs)
- Artists

In short, this list includes anyone who has something to teach, a skill to pass on, or a message to preach.

After using computer simulations for military purposes, Abt realized that the types of simulations used by the military could be used elsewhere. "Political and social situations," he said in *Serious Games*, "can often be viewed as games. Every election is a game. And almost all business activity is a game. Whether these contests of politics, war, economics, and interpersonal relations are played with resources of power, skill, knowledge, or luck, they always have the common characteristics of reciprocal decisions among independent actors with at least partly conflicting objectives."

As we cover the various markets for serious games in Part 2 of this book, we will provide examples of what has been done in those markets and what people in those markets are looking to achieve in the future.

Conclusion

When considering the educational value of books and movies, it has been observed that those books and movies that attempt to preach less have the greater effect. That is, the intended moral or meaning of a story is often ignored when blatantly stated. The effect is much greater when the message is instead woven into the characters, setting, and plots in an almost incidental, matter-of-fact manner.

Serious games offer a new mechanism for teaching and training by combining video games with education. Serious games can extend the value of training films and books by allowing the player to not only learn, but also to demonstrate and apply what he or she has learned.

Normally, game designers are not educators and educators are not game designers. The results of one group attempting to operate on their own within the domain of the other are seldom exemplary (though exceptions exist). However, by combining the skills of game designers with those of educators, serious games can be a force in teaching students of all ages.

Now that we've covered the basics of what serious games are, in the next chapter we will talk about design and development considerations game developers might face while working on serious games.

CHAPTER 3

SERIOUS GAMES DESIGN AND DEVELOPMENT ISSUES

Serious games are still games and therefore share many of the same design considerations and development issues as other video games. The techniques game designers use in entertainment games are quite transferable. In fact, game developers may have a competitive edge because many of the processes and technology are similar. However, significant differences exist, caused by the shift in goal from entertainment to education.

For example, one of the most common differences concerns the simulation of real world effects and processes. In an entertainment video game, the effect or process only needs to be "close enough" to approximate the desired result and, more importantly, to preserve the fun. In a serious game, though, the precise, real-world effects might be of overwhelming importance. In the military, this is especially true, but it also applies to medicine, emergency response, and any other case where lives are affected through the training. In these types of serious games, reality trumps fun.

In addition, there are several issues that video game designers and developers probably would not have encountered in their entertainment products. Examples include integration with an existing course curriculum, testing and assessment, and support for the assignment of specific tasks and/or "homework." For serious games to become a real tool of educators and trainers, these issues must be addressed.

Video game industry practices also have other assumptions that need to be avoided or at least carefully considered before including them or the features based on those assumptions. We will cover all of these issues in this chapter as well as look at the importance of fun in serious games.

HOW DO SERIOUS GAMES DIFFER FROM ENTERTAINMENT GAMES?

Note

"Don't try and peel the icing off the video game cake and lay it over the liver of learning and expect it to taste the same."

—David Thomas, of Buzzcut.com, in commentary
about the first Serious Games Summit

In the Serious Games survey (see Appendix B, "Serious Games Survey Results"), game developers who had worked on both entertainment and serious game projects were asked, "How has working on a serious game project differed from working on a retail game project?" The responses ranged from "not much at all" to "utterly different." Depending on your background in game development, the information presented in this chapter may seem closer to one extreme than the other.

Despite some similarities, serious games are different from entertainment games. Designers and developers must keep these differences in mind. They may have to challenge assumptions carried over from the retail arena and build support for aspects of serious games that they may have never encountered before.

Design Considerations: Assumptions to Avoid

For those designers and developers entrenched in the retail video game industry, they may have to *un*-learn some of the assumptions that drive the industry. Not only can the designer *not* (in most cases) count on designing and building the game for the "cutting edge" of hardware and software, he or she must also be prepared to accept that bigger isn't always better and that "what's fun" might not actually be what's needed to make the serious game a success.

The Latest and Greatest Hardware Is . . . Probably Unavailable

Much has been written about the "core market" for video games and its tendency to own the latest and greatest in hardware, software, and peripherals. Hardcore players, the target market for most retail games, demand games that help them justify their hardware, software, and peripheral purchases. As such, retail entertainment games made for the core market attempt to push new hardware to its limits and often run only passably well (if at all) on older hardware.

In contrast, many of the markets for serious games have less-than-optimal computers, often years old. Schools and corporations prefer to make the best use of what they have rather than invest in all new computers every year. And even if they have newer computers, these systems probably do not include many of the multi-media features used by the core gamer market, such as hardware-accelerated 3D graphics rendering, sophisticated sound cards with stereo speakers and subwoofers, high-capacity hard drives with dozens or hundreds of gigabytes of available storage, and so forth.

In addition to less modern equipment, many of these markets are likely to possess a wide variety of hardware and operating systems. Few organizations are completely homogenous in their IT systems, and it may be necessary for the serious game to be played simultaneously on computers varying in age, hardware, and capabilities.

Some serious games will require the latest and greatest hardware and software, but the developer shouldn't assume that will be the case for all serious games.

Similarly, the developer shouldn't assume that the target market for serious games includes only gamers. Many professionals in education and training, as well as many corporate executives and decision makers, have little or no experience with video games. So designers may have to go beyond the "industry standard" user interfaces, with all of their built-in assumptions about experienced players, and make their games even *more* accessible to possible first-time game players.

Bigger Isn't Necessarily Better

Since hardcore players tend to delight in bigger explosions, faster AI, and more immersive worlds, it's easy to fall into the idea that bigger is better. Hardcore gamers want the richest possible experience from their games, which means that those games must include gigabytes of content. Serious games, though, may be severely limited by available resources and the constraints of serious game design. For smaller serious games in particular, the time and budget to create a vast quantity of content may not be available.

The audience's broader base of computer hardware and software also limits what's possible and thus, bigger isn't always better in serious game development.

Furthermore, while accurate simulation is obviously important, too realistic of a simulation can be a mistake. Beyond the cost of creating or licensing the necessary technology, "ultimate realism" may get in the way of the overall usefulness of the resulting serious game. Michael Schrage, in *Serious Play: How the World's Best Companies Simulate to Innovate*, gave an example from a 1969 *Harvard Business Review* article (written by George Gershefski). The Corporate Economic Planning group at Sun Oil Company built a simulation with this goal: If you could manage Sun Oil's simulation, you could manage Sun Oil. It took 13 man-years to develop and 10 man-years to create management awareness. Every possible variable was accounted for. In the end, however, the managers never used the simulation. It was way too complicated. Later interviewed by Schrage, Gershefski said, "There was no need or demand for what the model could do; we had a screwdriver and we were running around looking for a screw." Schrage compared this project to a mapmaker making a map with a perfect 1:1 ratio. Certainly, such a large and detailed map would cover all the necessary information, but it's unlikely anyone would use or even need this map. "The proper question," Schrage wrote, "is not 'How will this model or simulation solve the problem?' but rather 'How will this simulation or model be used to solve the problem?'"

In *Rules of Play,* the authors Katie Salen and Eric Zimmerman stated, "A simulation can never contain every possible aspect of the phenomena being simulated. Historical wargaming has been wrestling with this challenge for at least a century."

The art of game design is as much about what is left out as it is what is put in. "Design is what happens when you work within constraints," said Kent Quirk, CEO of CogniToy, an independent game developer and a serious game subcontractor for the Defense Acquisition University. Serious game developers must make the choice of what to leave out so that the game focuses on only the most important elements needed to be taught or trained.

Think through Assumptions

Simulation models are just that: models. They attempt to recreate, in a controlled manner, what is often an incredibly complex system. In entertainment titles, a simulation can be "good enough." As long as the results of the simulation seem to match up with reality most of the time and the resulting game is deemed fun, "good enough" is, in fact, good enough.

In serious games, though, the simulation is often the beating heart of the game. What the player/trainee learns from the game is affected by how the game responds to his or her decisions and actions. Because the game should focus on the most important elements of training, the developer needs to be careful in determining the rules behind the simulation.

The simplification and definite rules of simulation models are one of their greatest strengths, but they are also the potential source of the greatest weaknesses. Assumptions *must* be made for the simulation to be workable. But if the wrong assumptions are chosen, the simulation breaks or worse. "Worse" is if the simulation teaches the wrong kinds of skills.

Referring again to Schrage, in *Serious Play* he talked about one of the main sources for such wrong assumptions: cultural taboos and blind spots. For example, in war games of the 1980s, the U.S. Navy would not allow aircraft carriers to be sunk in the simulation because it was commonly believed to be highly improbable, even though a British carrier was sunk by Argentina during the Falklands War. "There is a difference, of course, between hypotheses that are taboo because they contradict cherished beliefs and those that are dismissed because they're considered wildly unlikely.... But managers sometimes kid themselves about likelihoods. After all, the Titanic did sink."

Shortcuts for Fun May Not Apply

In entertainment games, simulations use a number of techniques to simplify the process being simulated and focus the game, and the player, on the "fun parts." In serious games, developers might have to avoid or rethink the use of these simulation shortcuts. A list of the more common techniques is as follows:

Common Simulation Shortcuts

- Random Numbers
- Time Compression
- Process Simplification
- Headache Removal
- Perfect Communication

Random numbers are used to great effect in most, if not all, games. Random results have proven useful for everything from keeping computer AI unpredictable to creating 3D forests for the player to explore. In serious games, however, random numbers need to be used carefully. "No serious game can be successful," Abt said, "if the players do not understand its rules, their objectives in the game, the consequences of their action, and the reasons for these consequences. In this sense, serious games should differ from more conventional games. They should respond more to the conscious decisions of the players than to an outside element of chance." Therefore, a game like *Monopoly* would not make a good serious game teaching real estate investment because winning depends more on dice rolls than on decisions made by the players.

Time compression removes or reduces the amount of downtime between an action and its reaction. For example, in real-time strategy (RTS) games, troops respond immediately to all orders given. There is no (or very little) time lag between the order and the unit's beginning to act on that order. In a real battle, however, the order might have to be transmitted via the chain of command, through several middlemen, resulting in a latency between giving the order and the action happening.

Time compression also happens in other ways. Battles that would take days are resolved in seconds, and year-long campaigns happen in minutes or hours. In this case, time compression helps the player to focus on what is important to the simulation, and combined with process simplification, turns a complex, time-consuming task into a game. If a simulation is intended to be real-time, time compression might not be an option.

Process simplification removes or reduces steps in the process that are tedious or otherwise "not fun." Driving games, for instance, often greatly simplify the process of driving with a manual transmission. The coordination of putting the transmission in gear, giving the engine gas, and letting go of the clutch is not easily simulated on most computers, and would make the game more challenging to new players. Games usually draw the player in with simplicity, only adding complexity when the player has mastered the current level. With a stick shift, the learning process is very front-loaded.

Another example of this occurs in many retail first-person shooter (FPS) games where car doors provide protection from enemy gunfire. This assumption simplifies the search for and simulation of "hard cover" (cover that hides the soldier and also provides protection), but real soldiers and police officers readily attest to the folly of seeking cover behind an open car door.

Headache removal is a form of process simplification that gets rid of or minimizes problems and issues that can happen in the situation being simulated. Such problems, though authentic, usually add little more than frustration for a player, and so the game designer wisely eliminates them. In a serious game, though, it might be important for the player to learn how to deal with the frustration. Having a gun jam in combat due to a faulty firing mechanism or ammunition is a very real, and potentially deadly, headache that still afflicts modern weapons. Video games seldom simulate gun jamming, except when it seems dramatically useful, because it's just not fun. Players don't put up with equipment in a game that doesn't work as expected. In a serious game, though, learning how to deal with such issues could be an important part of the process.

Flight simulators are built around this very concept. Flight simulators are often "crash and malfunction" simulators. The instructors hit the pilot trainee with everything from a fire in the wiring to doors falling off at high altitudes.

Perfect communication is a combination of time compression, process simplification, and headache removal. In the real world, communication is seldom perfect. Referring to RTS games again, the commander gives an order and the troops begin to carry out the order immediately and exactly as given. In a real battle, however, there is a chain of command and the very real chance that the orders might be misunderstood and/or passed along incorrectly. "Friendly fire" is one of the more obvious examples of imperfect communication.

A serious game might choose to use any of the above simulation shortcuts, but the decision on which one to use or avoid varies according to the goals of the serious game.

Testing and Integration

Serious games have additional considerations that distinguish them from entertainment games. Chief among these is testing and learning feedback. Trainers and educators need to know whether or not the player has actually learned the content of the serious game. Furthermore, they must be able to integrate the serious game with their existing curriculum and teaching methods.

Testing

The culture of video games, both in making them and in playing them, is very different from the cultures of education and training. For serious games to be accepted into the various cultures of education, designers of serious games must learn to bridge the distance between those cultures and the video game culture.

Modern education is built around the concept of mastering (and/or memorizing) designated content, progressing through a number of school levels (primary, secondary, college, etc.) until finally graduating with a diploma or degree. Even outside the field of education, corporate and military training works within a similar structure. Material is presented to the students/ trainees, and their mastery of that material is tested in various ways before they get credit for learning the material.

For serious games to be considered a useful tool to educators and trainers, they must provide testing and progress tracking. The results of the testing must be recognizable within the context of the education or training.

Many retail games have already built in a simple mechanism for tracking progress: game levels. Well-designed games start out with the simplest levels, with each following level building on those game features and strategies introduced in the earlier levels. In a sense, successfully completing a level demonstrates mastery of what the game has "taught" so far.

Testing is not limited to *following* the material presented, however. In some cases, especially when still developing or prototyping the serious game, it may be necessary to test the students and trainees beforehand to see what they already know. That way, the teachers have a valid sample of their students' existing knowledge or skills to compare with what the students have learned after playing the serious game. The serious game needs to be able to show this proof of learning.

To facilitate testing, serious games need to include

- Extensive, detailed logging of all player choices and actions
- Review/replay controls
- Easy customizing of material to be tested on, with set goals

In addition, testing is not limited to a reproduction of facts, which is frequently the case in education. A willing student can often ace such a test through rote memorization without even fully understanding all the issues involved. Serious games provide an opportunity to test beyond Q&A or multiple choice and may be uniquely suited to demonstrating processes, interactions, systems, causes, and consequences. Abt, in *Serious Games*, suggested the following criteria in judging the usefulness of a serious game:

- Active involvement and stimulation of all players
- Sufficient realism to convey the essential truths of the simulation
- Clarity of consequences and their causes in both rules and gameplay
- Repeatability and reliability of the entire process

It may seem like some desired results, such as improved decision-making, would be hard to measure. However, improved decision-making can definitely be tracked over the progress of the game. If presented with similar situations, the trainee can incorporate earlier learning (or "mistakes") to react more appropriately. Ideally, a serious game would track such metrics so that trainers can gauge the progress of students.

Integration

Serious games are expected to *assist* teachers, not *replace* them. Serious games, therefore, need to be integrated into the education process. Testing for mastery of the material is only one aspect of that process. Though this section may seem to apply primarily to teachers in the traditional classroom, training programs of all varieties already have lesson plans and established curriculum. For serious games to be useful in these situations, they must be designed to facilitate lesson plans.

Many of the features for testing discussed earlier would also be useful in utilizing the serious game in the classroom. In addition to detailed logging, reviewing, and customizing, other features to consider are

- Observer modes for both teachers and other students

- Coaching options (from observer mode)

- Pause/play options to quickly suspend/resume the game

Most game developers are familiar with observer modes, which allow uninvolved players to "observe" the game as played by someone else. Most often, the game is presented to the observer exactly as the player sees it. Coaching options would extend the observer mode by allowing the observer varying levels of interaction with the player. The type of options possible range from simple instruction (via voice chat or typed text) to changing the effect of player decisions or even changing parts of the simulation or situation as it's running.

Since school budgets often limit the number of computers available to less (sometimes significantly less) than the number of students, serious games might be played by groups of students. One student directly plays the game, as the others watch and provide suggestions. Or the teacher might prefer to present the serious game to the class all at once, either playing it alone or with a designated student doing the "driving" while the other students watch and participate vocally. In these situations, the ability to pause the game to solicit feedback from the class or the other players facilitates cooperation and communication.

Education often extends past the boundaries of the classroom and the facility through homework. Though the ultimate benefits of homework have been debated extensively over the last century, homework has become a staple of modern education. Serious games that target education should expect to support the assignment and handling (especially grading) of homework. Such support could include

- Easy creation of assignments with set goals

- A mechanism for submitting completed homework

The creation of actual lesson plans that use serious games in the classroom will almost certainly need to be done by educators and not game designers. To that end, the suite of "modding" tools created to accompany the serious game will need to be well-documented and easy for non-gamers (teachers and educators) to use.

In addition to the creation or "modding" aspects, there should be tools to support the collection, grading, and review of homework assignments. For a teacher, the review and grading of homework is one of the most time-consuming chores of teaching. Each day, a teacher with a class of 30 students must collect assigned work from the 30 students and save them for review. After the review, the 30 assignments must then be returned to the students so they can gauge how well they did.

Any assistance the game designer can provide in the design to facilitate this review is likely to be both welcome and necessary to speed the adoption of the serious game.

ADDITIONAL DESIGN ISSUES

There are a couple final design issues that we want to touch on. First, is it important, or even useful, for serious games to be fun? And, finally, fun or not, how do you get the players to actually play the serious games?

Importance of Fun

How important is fun to serious games? Is it necessary, or even desirable for serious games to be fun? These games are, by definition, intended for the very serious task of teaching. Can there be room for fun in education?

The whole point of edutainment was to make education entertaining, thereby motivating students to learn on their own. However, the uneven track record of edutainment, especially in classroom settings, has made some educators wary and unsure if they trust anything that smacks of fun. To a very real extent, this goes back to the necessity of testing how much is learned from serious games. Visible, repeatable results will do more to convince the skeptics than anything else.

Whether a serious game *should* be fun, though, isn't an easy question. Some subject matter doesn't translate well into the fun arena of entertainment games. For example, how important is it that a game training people on how to respond to emergency medical situations also be fun?

The main argument in favor of instilling fun into serious games is that it helps motivate the players to play (and learn) on their own. Michael Bean, of the business simulation company Forio, wrote in his online article, "What Makes a Simulation Fun," "This idea of people motivated to learn on their own explains why simulations aren't just another activity to embed into a workshop. They can literally change the way people learn. If a simulation is fun, the simulation takes on a life of its own."

As mentioned before, in a survey (see survey result 3.1) of serious game developers, educators, and researchers done for this book, over 80 percent of respondents said that "element of fun" was Important or Very Important.

Though hardly a survey of the entire serious games industry, it does seem interesting that no one rated "fun" as "Not Important." Even when the goal of the game isn't entertainment, fun can't be totally discounted.

Serious Games Survey Result 3.1

Question: How do you rate the importance of the "element of fun" in serious games?

33.33%	Very Important
47.62%	Important
15.87%	Useful, but not a primary goal
3.17%	Less Important
0.00%	Not Important

(Survey Note: 63 Respondents)

Getting Players to Play

When games are in the day's lesson plan, getting students to play them is as simple as assigning them as work. The students pass or fail according to how they did or didn't do the assignment. The motivation of the students scarcely enters the equation. But what if the students want to play the serious game, even on their own time? This is an ideal situation.

In that case, the "people play and learn from [the simulations]," Bean wrote, "without being compelled to." And "without realizing it, they develop and internalize rules for success that they can intuitively apply in the real world."

As we discussed in Chapter 2, it's possible for entertainment to also be educational, which is one of the reasons why we are studying serious games in the first place. The reverse is also true, though, and "fun" isn't the only form of entertainment, nor the only way to hook player interest in a game. At the movies, documentaries have audiences even though such films are not as "fun" as the latest blockbuster. At the bookstore, there are hundreds of thousands of new books available each year, many of them non-fiction. Talk radio holds its own against the music-only radio stations. The growth of cable TV has created an explosion of informational programming and channels. So "fun" isn't the only game in town.

People become motivated to learn on their own when they can relate to what's being taught and see how it affects their lives. When combined with easily customized content, serious games could be created to reflect the specific region, city, school, or place of business where the student/trainee/player resides. A business simulation can include information about actual clients. A physics lab simulation can show how the lab experiments translate into the real world. A political game can show how elections or policies can affect the local region, or even the world.

People like to see themselves and hear about themselves. Show them *themselves* and *their world* in the game, and they'll want to play.

CONCLUSION

Serious games are both games—and not games. They are games insofar as they have rules, simulate behaviors, accept input from the player, and provide feedback within the context of the rules and behaviors. As such, serious games have many of the same design issues as entertainment games.

However, since the primary design criteria is not "fun," serious games are also very different from entertainment games. In serious games, "fun" takes a backseat. Instead, the accuracy of the process or effect being simulated for training is of primary importance. In addition to the accuracy of what's being taught, the serious game must also be concerned with *whether* —and *what*—the game is actually teaching the player. If the player learns to beat the game but can't usefully apply what he's learned in the real world, then the serious game has failed in its mission.

Serious games also need to be easily integrated into existing lesson plans and course material because they are a teaching tool and not substitutes for teachers and trainers. So designers and developers need to make sure their serious games are adaptable to a variety of classroom and training situations as well as being easy to use.

This concludes Part 1. In Part 2 of the book, we will cover the various markets that are interested in funding, developing, and using serious games.

Part

2

Serious Game Markets

Though there has been an increase in attention given to serious games, they are hardly new. Like entertainment-oriented video games, video games with a serious bent have been around as long as computers have been around to run them.

The first such games were more often called "simulations" because they were designed to simulate battlefield and business situations. Generals and CEOs would use their investments in million-dollar computer hardware and software to model how various strategies and tactics might play out in the real world. Despite the high price tag, these simulations allowed for significant savings in both human and material resources. As computers and their software became simultaneously less expensive and more powerful, the possibilities for simulation expanded.

Video games and simulations have traditionally followed separate but parallel development tracks. Both strive to duplicate reality in a convincing manner, but simulations need to be as "real" as possible. In the past, simulations were cutting-edge investments designed to be run on the most powerful computers and display devices available. Meanwhile, video games got by with what technology was available on the market and later targeted the audience of personal computers. Beginning in the 1990s, though, with the explosion in 3D technology and real-time rendering techniques, the two paths started to converge. Video game technology is now sufficient for many applications.

Military-grade simulations still target the high-end, but there is also a move to use "off-the-shelf" components in both software and hardware. For non-military applications, off-the-shelf technology and games are proving adequate, opening up possibilities for other agencies and organizations whose budgets don't claim significant percentages of the Gross National Product.

In Part 2, we will cover each of the primary markets for serious games: the military, the government, education, corporations, and healthcare. The government, especially the military, has been the primary source of funding for serious games. This trend will likely continue but corporations and other groups with training and education needs are also increasing their budgets for serious games.

For each of these markets, we will cover the following:

- The history of serious games used within the market

- How serious games are currently being used

- How serious games will be used in the future.

Then we will go into depth about developing serious games for these markets, covering

- Market expectations for serious games

- Requirements for developers looking to work on serious games in this market

- Special requirements for the particular market (e.g., security clearance for military projects, or patient privacy issues for healthcare).

In addition to the primary markets listed above, we will also cover serious games produced by and for religious groups, political activists, and multimedia artists. The budgets for these markets are often significantly smaller than those for government agencies or corporations. Many serious games have already been created within these diverse areas, however, and interest in serious games is expected to grow.

Chapter 4, "Military Games," covers the military, currently the largest source of serious game funding and research. The main emphasis is on the United States military branches, but the military organizations of other countries are also interested in serious games.

Chapter 5, "Government Games," then looks at the rest of the government agencies that have used serious games. Such agencies include the Department of Homeland Security, the Department of the Interior, and more. Even at the state and local levels, there are government agencies interested in serious games.

Chapter 6, "Educational Games," looks at education. At both the national and local levels, educators are paying more attention to this new teaching medium and looking for ways to effectively use serious games in their classrooms.

Chapter 7, "Corporate Games," shifts the emphasis from the public sector to the private sector and examines serious games in the corporate space. Corporations, big and small, are investing in serious games for both training and planning.

In Chapter 8, "Healthcare Games," we'll look at how serious games are being used in healthcare for treatment, recovery, and rehabilitation. The use of serious games in healthcare also includes mental health.

Chapter 9, "Political, Religious, and Art Games," covers the broad spectrum of political, religious, and art games. These games often intend to spread a message more than teach the players, but that's still a form of education.

Concluding with Chapter 10, "Final Thoughts," we'll discuss the future of serious games.

MILITARY GAMES

The military has perhaps the longest history of using games to teach new recruits and new officers. Chess, with origins dating back to the 7th century, is one of the most well known military training games. Though highly stylized, chess is considered one of the best representations of warfare in the pregunpowder age. Officers-in-training were taught chess in hopes of improving their performance on the battlefield. Yet even chess was based on still earlier wargames, going back thousands of years, so there can be little doubt that warfare and games go hand in hand.

According to authors Dunnigan and Perla, the modern wargame developed in the 17th century. These games started as simple variations of chess, updating the playing pieces to reflect contemporary military units and adding more complex terrain. Over the next couple centuries, though, much more sophisticated and complex simulations evolved, many of which required copious statistics and tables covering a myriad of possibilities. Unlike chess, few of these games ever "crossed over" into the civilian world as entertainment.

In World War II, the development of computational machines, the earliest computers, birthed the period we're interested in for this book. In this chapter, we will review a brief history of wargames and the use of computer games for military simulation. We will also cover some of what is happening today and provide a peek into what the future holds.

Then we will cover the peculiarities of developing for the military. To that end, we will cover the basics of developing games for the military, starting with issues of sensitive information, national secrets, and security clearances. Then we will go over programs created to assist with the funding of serious games for military applications. Along the way, we will review several case studies of developers who have worked for the military in various capacities.

Serious Games in the Military

Many games are simulations, abstractions of some element or elements of physical reality. There are rules and boundaries, and mastery of the rules of the game can, with proper guidance, be transferred from the abstract universe of the game back into the concrete, real world. This transfer is the basis for interest in serious games in general, and the main reason the military has for centuries been interested in wargames as an inexpensive (in both men and resources) way to train new officers.

Wargames, Simulations, and the Cold War

Chess is considered by many to be the original wargame, but it's not. In *The Art of Wargaming*, Peter Perla traced the origins of modern chess to a four-sided board game called *Chaturanga* played by the nobility of India over four millennia ago. *Chaturanga* is thought to have developed at or around the same time ("give or take a thousand years") as the Chinese game *Wei Hei* that evolved into the classic Japanese game *Go*.

Prehistory aside, learning chess in the centuries before gunpowder provided a way for the newly minted officers of the aristocracy to see how the different troops available to them could be used. This learning, limited though it was by the simple rules and interactions of the pieces, at least allowed those officers to go into their battles with a plan. The old adage that "no battle plan survives contact with the enemy" would mean that the plan changed during implementation, but even that minimal amount of preparation could mean the difference between victory and defeat.

The condensed reality of a game removes distractions that might otherwise get in the way of insights that can be applied in the real world. By utilizing the game of chess, a commander can experiment with different strategies to understand how they might play out in real life without risking any of his troops or other resources. By seeing the whole "battlefield" at a glance, he doesn't get distracted and bogged down by one, possibly inconsequential, aspect of the conflict and can focus on creating an overall battle plan.

The other way that wargames help commanders is by pitting them against another living, breathing commander. The interaction of plan and counterplan provides a chance for the commander to learn about holes in his strategy that he hasn't perceived. The other player is also trying to win, and so looks for weaknesses to exploit.

The Growth of Complexity

The value of mastery and insight depends very much on how well the game simulates the reality it's based on. For that reason, most modern wargames do not have the simplicity and ease of play represented by chess. Chess has only six different playing pieces (king, queen, bishop, rook, knight, and pawn) and a simple 2-color, 8 x 8 grid as a playing board (see Figure 4.1). Though each of the six pieces has its own rules of movement and attack, compared to the complex simulations used by the Prussian military in the 19th century, chess is childlike in its simplicity.

Kriegspiel, designed in the first half of the 19th century by Lieutenant George Heinrich Rudolph Johann von Reisswitz and based on a wargame designed by his father, Baron von Reisswitz, had a longer military career than its creator. The game used topographical maps drawn at 1:8000 scale and metal strips to represent troops. Through an umpire, the game maintained the "fog of war," showing only those troops on the map that could be seen by the combatants.

After Prussian victories in the "Six Weeks War" against Austria in 1866 and the Franco-Prussian War of 1870–1871, the rest of the world took notice of the Kriegspiel. Military men in other countries began to examine the Kriegspiel, modifying it to match their own training needs and to keep the game current with modern weapons.

As complex as these Kriegspiel-inspired wargames were, however, wargames were destined to become even more complicated. Accounting for such weapons as machine guns, tanks, fighter aircraft, bombers, aircraft carriers, and tactics like combined arms and command and control, and more, the level of complexity rose to unforeseen heights.

In typical modern wargames, the rules of movement for the variety of weapons and troops available, the charts for determining the outcome of conflicts between individual units, and accounting for each of the varying terrain and encounter situations, can require enough pages of text and charts to fill a textbook. The changing focus of military operations from the destruction of enemy forces to a focus on the destruction of the enemy's ability to fight has added even more cases that must be adjudicated. Playing such a wargame, even a single battle, can take hours or even days, as players consult those rules and charts to position and move their units, and then resolve encounters between units.

Computers at War

With such complexity of interaction and judging, computers are a natural fit for wargames. Computers provide both an impartial referee and an untiring "rules gopher" who ensures that the players follow the situation-appropriate rules of movement, weapon effects, physical laws, and so on. Civilian wargames caught on to this natural fit as soon as minicomputers and microcomputers (personal computers) became available. The military, however, including the U.S. military, took a bit longer.

After World War II, the U.S. military's use of computer wargames was largely limited to "operations research" (OR) at the strategic level. Operations research is a type of systems analysis that brings modern science, mathematics, and statistics to bear on solving a particular problem. In this particular case, the problem was defense in a nuclear age. One of the most widely used OR-based computer simulations was *ATLAS*, developed by the Department of Defense (DoD) in the early 1960s and used into the 1980s.

Also in the 1960s, at the Advanced Studies Department of the Raytheon Missile Systems Division, a team designed computer simulations of air battles, space missions, missile exchanges, disarmament inspection systems, and international political-economic competitions.

The first Persian Gulf War and the breakup of the Soviet Union in the latter part of the 20th century, along with the explosive growth of realistic 3D rendering in video games, brought about the beginning of the end of the old approach and a focus on new methods. Before discussing these new methods, though, we will examine the military's use of another game-like tool: the simulator.

Simulators—the Other Wargames

Simulators, especially vehicle simulators, have long been a staple of military training. Flight simulators are perhaps the bestknown example of how the military uses highly accurate simulations to train personnel. If you don't think of flight simulators as being games, consider the millions of copies of *Microsoft Flight Simulator* sold over the years, as well as the popularity of more entertainment-oriented flight game series, like *Falcon* and *Comanche*.

Though flight simulators are considered a necessary step in pilot training today, it took over two decades before they were accepted as a viable way to train new pilots. As pilot and command experience with aircraft in war grew, it was observed that in wartime, the death rates of pilots correlated with the number of sorties they had flown. For a new pilot, the first run was the most dangerous. As a pilot flew more and more missions, the likelihood of death decreased. If seasoned veterans of skirmishes could learn how to survive through experience, then flight simulators could allow trainees to become "virtual veterans" and become better prepared for problems in flight. Therefore, all flight training today, military or otherwise, involves hundreds of hours in simulators before the new pilot is allowed to take the control of a real aircraft.

The earliest flight simulators, built from before World War I and into the late 1920s, were purely mechanical or pneumatic. Skeptics abounded, questioning the efficacy of the chunky, odd-looking devices. It wasn't until instruments-only flying and navigation became important that the true value of flight simulators was seen. Instruments-only training in a flight simulator proved much safer, for everyone involved (and nearby), than similar training in a real plane touching down on a real runway.

World War II, with its need to train large numbers of pilots quickly, pushed the development of flight simulators further, as did the subsequent Cold War requirements of the military and the growing commercial airline industry. Over the years, simulators have been enhanced. First, analog computers (or differential analyses, as they were known at the time) were added, and then digital computers. More recently, networking capabilities have provided flight simulators, and other vehicle simulators, with many new options and training possibilities.

In the 1980s, the military began networking its simulators together to make it possible for trainees to be operating in the same battle space, both as opponents and as teams. With that change, according to Col. Matthew Caffrey, USAF Reserves, a Professor at Air Command Staff College, simulators went from being purely procedural trainers to being tactical trainers.

Today, everyone agrees that flight simulators are useful training tools. Further-more, simulators are an ideal way to make sure a pilot's skills are kept up to date.

The military utilizes more than just fixed-wing aircraft and helicopter simulators. There are also tank simulators, humvee simulators, and more. If it can be piloted or driven, the modern military has a simulator to train soldiers in its operation and the network infrastructure to train them in groups.

Modern Training for Modern Wars

To say that the military, particularly the United States military, is "interested" in video games for training is to make an incredible understatement. The "President's Budget Request for Fiscal Year 2003, National Defense Section" specified $10 billion for training. For the Pentagon, simulation equipment and wargames take up $4 billion a year. To further demonstrate the military's commitment to training games, the United States encouraged other NATO members to use games for training at a conference in October 2004 called Exploiting Commercial Games For Military Use.

Recruiting and Beyond

In 2002, the U.S. Army created *America's Army*. Based on Epic's *Unreal Tournament* engine, *America's Army* has proven to be one of the most successful military recruiting tools ever. The U.S. Army needed to put 80,000 new volunteer soldiers "in boots" every year, and the game has proven surprisingly successful at doing just that and at 15 percent of the cost of other recruiting programs.

An Army survey to assess its recruiting effectiveness found that among young adults, age 16–24, the game had given them more of a positive impression than any other Army recruiting endeavors. The Army intends to do long-term studies with new recruits to ascertain if the skills learned in *America's*

Army are retained after basic training and if the game can be used to direct career choices within the Army.

In the fall of 2004, *America's Army* had been downloaded over 17 million times, had a community of 4 million registered players (both civilian and military), with 100,000 new players joining the game each month. In addition, 30 percent of *America's Army* players are not in America but in other countries, like Sweden, Germany, and France. In this way, *America's Army* serves as a goodwill ambassador by promoting core American values.

According to Col. Casey Wardynski (see Figure 4.2), Director of the U.S. Army's Office of Economic Manpower Analysis (OEMA) and the Army manager who oversaw the development of the game, one of the main goals of *America's Army* was verisimilitude, to be as real as it gets. "The next best thing," Col. Wardynski said in an interview, "would be to be a real soldier." Though the game does sacrifice some realism in the name of entertainment (e.g., you can be safe hiding behind cars in the game; don't try this in Iraq), the feel of the game is undeniably realistic and gritty.

Even if the authenticity of *America's Army* dissuades potential recruits, it will have some benefit. In the past, an estimated 13.7 percent of new recruits would drop out before completing basic training, costing the Army an average of $15,000 per person in wasted investment. By showing what it takes to get through basic training and beyond, *America's Army* appeals to

FIGURE 4.2

Col. Casey Wardynski, Director of the U.S. Army's Office of Economic Manpower Analysis (OEMA)

© Sande Chen. Used with Permission

the ones who are more likely to succeed in the Army and dissuades those who might not have the wherewithal to finish boot camp.

Beyond its recruiting uses, however, *America's Army* has also helped to *pre-train* new recruits. Since its release, many of the new recruits arriving at Fort Benning, Georgia, are already familiar with the layout of the training camp and with a general understanding of how training will proceed. In addition to detailed and accurate settings, like Ft. Benning, uniforms and weaponry in the game are as authentic as possible.

In 2003, the Army expanded the brand by releasing *America's Army: Special Forces* (see Figure 4.3) to highlight the role of elite forces and in 2005, partnered with Ubisoft for *America's Army: Rise of a Soldier*, the console version available for PlayStation2 and Xbox.

Since its initial release, *America's Army* has also been modified and extended to be a training tool used by more than potential recruits. Active soldiers have used the game to prepare for missions and even to practice defusing bombs. Furthermore, the *America's Army* Future Applications team uses the *America's Army* Platform to prototype future weapons systems, like the XM25 Air Burst Weapon System. By repurposing *America's Army* in these

FIGURE 4.3

Authentic uniform and weaponry in America's Army: Special Forces

© United States Army. Used with Permission

additional ways, the Army has realized significant time and cost saving on its initial investment. For example, the TALON robot trainer currently in use took a mere 2–3 months to develop at a cost of $60,000 by building it as an extension of *America's Army*. Previously, soldiers would have had to be brought to a training location to be trained on new equipment, but with the TALON robot trainer within *America's Army*, instructors can put it on a laptop and take the training anywhere.

The military's interest in serious games extends beyond its own, highly specialized, often very expensive versions of such games. The entertainment-driven video games available at retail have also proven useful to the military, and those games, and the people who play them, have become the focus of a lot of attention.

The Video Game Generation

The military has discovered a host of benefits in a generation of recruits that grew up playing video games, in the arcade and at home. The most obvious of these is *improved hand-eye coordination*. Video games, especially those popular with young males, almost always include an element of "twitch," the ability to spot game state changes and respond quickly (see Figure 4.4). In fact, researchers at the University of Rochester have documented that players of "twitch" games are more efficient at processing fast-changing visual information. There are additional advantages that are all natural outgrowths of playing video games:

- **Improved ability to multitask.** In action-oriented video games, players have to keep track of many different things at once: where they are in the overall game, where they are in the current mission or level, where their teammates are, what type of resources they have available, the number and type of enemies and obstacles they have to overcome, and so on. To stay calm and controlled in chaotic circumstances is a useful skill in the military.

- **Improved target differentiation.** A key ability in combat situations is being able to correctly identify friend from foe so that you can shoot the latter without harming the former. Multiplayer FPS games, especially, have given players lots of practice at this.

- **Target prioritization.** Not only is it important to correctly pick out the enemy targets, it's also necessary to pick the correct (or more correct) enemy target to attack first. The realism of many video games has provided many opportunities to practice prioritizing targets. And unlike real life, in video games you get to practice this over and over.

- **Ability to work within a team using minimal communication.** When on a mission, it's imperative that members of the team communicate quickly and clearly. In multiplayer games, the number of communication options is often quite limited, and players have developed skills to overcome those limitations. They learn their role in the team and anticipate where they should be and where they are most needed. Also, they have experience in what information is useful to pass along to help their teammates make similar assessments.

- **Desensitization of shooting at human targets.** A side effect of having grown up with video games depicting highly realistic scenes and characters is that new soldiers are more desensitized to shooting at human targets than were the soldiers of previous generations.

- **Willingness to take aggressive action.** The die-reload-try-again cycle of video games has engendered in players an aggressive, charge-in-and-see-what-happens approach. Though the accompanying feeling of invincibility may not last longer than the first encounter with *live* ammunition, this practice in taking the initiative can be valuable in combat situations.

FIGURE 4.4

"Twitch" games develop skills needed in the military.

© Sande Chen.
Used with Permission

If a soldier can hone necessary skills during his leisure time, that would be ideal. According to military experts, soldiers with video game know-how have excelled at military tasks similar to video game playing, such as operating long-range unmanned robotic aircraft. In the future, unmanned robotic aircraft may be called upon to spy in enemy airspace and jam enemy air defense systems. Recently, the Defense Advanced Research Projects Agency (DARPA) awarded Boeing a $766.7 million contract to continue work on these aerial vehicles.

Modifying Video Games for War

The military has also shown an interest in commercial off-the-shelf (COTS) video games. In some cases, the game can be used in training as is. In others, the cost of modifying the game to meet the military's requirements is much more agreeable than commissioning an entirely new product. Michael Robel, in his Web article "The Difference Between Military and Civilian Wargames" lists a number of such games that are in use by the military:

- *TacOps*, published by Battlefront.com, is, according to its own marketing copy, ". . .a simulation of contemporary and near-future tactical, ground combat between United States (Army and Marine), Canadian, New Zealand/Australian, and German forces versus various opposing forces (OPFOR), simulating the former Soviet Union, China, North Korea, etc."

- *Brigade Combat Team*, published by Shrapnel Games, touts itself as "... a real-time strategy game that examines the complexities of fighting on the modern battlefield."

- *Decisive Action*, published by HPS Simulations, is ". . .a modern Division and Corps level simulation that depicts combat with maneuver brigades and battalions along with supporting artillery, air strikes, electronic warfare, engineer, helicopters, and even [psychological] units."

- *Harpoon 3,* published by Advanced Gaming Systems, is ". . .a real-time naval war game on an operational/tactical level. It accurately models and simulates naval and air warfare. Including most aspects of naval and air combat including editable platforms, sensors, and weapons." *Harpoon* was originally a miniatures wargame of the same name, published in 1979 by Adventure Games.

According to the Advanced Gaming Systems Web site, the Australian Defense Department funded the development of two variants of *Harpoon 3*. Earlier versions of the game were used by Brazilian War College, the U.S. Air Force Staff and Command School, and (unofficially) by the Netherlands, Greece, Turkey, United Kingdom, and Korea.

Other commercial games, like *WarCraft* by Blizzard Entertainment, have been modified for use by the military. In the past, the U.S. Marine Corps has used a mod of *Doom* and a special version of *Close Combat* for training. Similarly, the U.S. Air Force has used *Microsoft Flight Simulator*.

For today's needs, DARPA is funding DARWARS, which started in 2003, to enhance military training. Already, some of the systems developed are being used in the field, such as DARWARS *Ambush!* DARWARS *Ambush!*, a mod of *Operation Flashpoint*, addresses convoy survival training, an urgent need as the military continues its operations in Iraq and Afghanistan.

Non-Combat Training

Not all military training via games and game technology is combat-oriented. When deployed outside the U.S., for example, soldiers often find themselves in very different cultures and unable to speak the language. Various companies and university research programs are working to solve both of these problems.

In the fall of 2004, researchers at the Information Sciences Institute at the University of Southern California were working on *Tactical Iraqi*, a game-based effort to teach Arabic to U.S. soldiers (who most often know only a single language, English) before they ship out. These types of serious games involve work with speech recognition technology, since speaking a language is vitally important to learning it. A human facilitator monitors and corrects trainees, since the technology is still relatively new.

debriefings after the mission is completed. If the design of the simulation is engaging enough, it's not impossible to assume that soldiers would be willing to play the games in their off hours, combining unsupervised entertainment with training.

Noting the usefulness of multiplayer simulations, the military has been eyeing the potential of massively multiplayer online games (MMOGs). Robert Gehorsam, now C.E.O. of Forterra Systems, approached the military in 2002 with an idea for using technology from *There* to simulate "warfare against insurgents in urban settings." *There* is an MMOG that pays particular attention to realism, especially in regard to player avatars. The realism of virtual worlds makes MMOGs ideal for dealing with urban warfare situations, such as occupation and dealing with insurgencies. In October 2004, Joint Forces Command officials tested the waters by conducting the largest real-time computer urban warfare simulation in history with gamers at three different sites controlling up to 100,000 entities.

In a December 2004 *Military Simulation & Training* article examining the capabilities of MMOGs, Jason Robar of the AISA Group wrote, "It is clear that a technology that can host 600,000 concurrent players in an environment of competing guilds and clans, each a politico-military organization, has some military applications." MMOGs, he went on, "offer some compelling new capabilities that may be able to augment and enhance how warfighters and the intelligence community prepare and train for . . . the 21st century."

Live training operations, deploying hundreds or even thousands of military personnel into the field, have been a staple of military training for centuries. The cost of such operations, though, in terms of both men and equipment, makes them less than ideal. With MMOG technology bringing together troops from around the world, such operations can be done for much less expense and with much more secrecy.

In addition to MMOG technology, the military is contemplating virtual reality trainers. The U.S. Army has a $6 million program to develop "virtual-training technology" built on the experience of actual combat veterans. The program uses virtual reality-type technology, multiplayer environments, and even computerized mannequins to help train medical personnel. By incorporating the experience of veteran warfighters, new trainees can be presented with much more accurate simulations.

Training for the military has advanced significantly in the past decades, and serious games have played a large part in that advance. Though there are still many in command and training positions that distrust games as teaching tools, there can be little doubt that use of video games will become more important in the years to come.

With the increased focus on serious games, game designers and game developers can certainly be of use to the military. The next section of this chapter covers developing for the military.

DEVELOPING SERIOUS GAMES FOR THE MILITARY

To the experienced game developer, developing serious games for the military will be similar to developing games for the retail publishers in a number of ways:

- Long lead time in pitching the game and securing a contract and funding.

- The need to determine who owns the final product and associated intellectual property.

- The possibility of sudden project cancellation.

The differences, though, are not insignificant:

- More upfront paperwork, including the possible need for security clearances. Accurate timesheets, for example, detailing where each member of the development team is devoting his or her time are very important.

- An appeals process following awarding the contract, open to other companies who bid on the project.

- An emphasis on substance (precise simulation specifications) over style (movie-ready 3D rendering).

Also, military training games need to provide support for the three phases of mission training:

- **Preparation phase.** Assists with the planning of the mission.
- **Execution phase.** Trains participants in what's needed of them during the particular mission.
- **After-action review (AAR).** Provides both commanders and personnel direct feedback about the success (or failure) of the mission.

Most retail video games focus on the execution phase. The AAR, however, is particularly important, as it reviews what was *supposed* to happen, establishes what *actually* happened, determines what went *right* and *wrong*, and assists with determining how the mission could be *done better* in the future.

Sensitive Information, Top Secret Data, and Security Clearances

Contracts and non-disclosure agreements (NDAs) are hardly new to game developers. The developer and publisher sign a NDA agreeing not to give out designated company information and "trade secrets." They also sign a development contract listing all the agreed upon terms. For the military, though, NDAs are only the beginning, and the very process to get a development contract is subject to certain rules.

Sensitive Information

When you deal with the government, and especially with the military, you need to be aware that you may be safeguarding sensitive information. "Loose lips sink ships" has been a military truism for at least a century now, and in our post-9/11 age, we need to take this issue very seriously.

A potential breach of security in the military sector has a much greater impact than in the private business sector. In the private sector, you run the risk of lawsuits and maybe criminal proceedings, but in the military sector, there could be national or even international consequences. And never forget: The military, by definition, is the group with the guns. Lots of guns. If *they* take sensitivity of information seriously, so should you.

While not all development contracts will require security screening, developers interested in pursuing military contracts should be aware of the possibility. Security screening of civilian contractors is quite common in regard to the military. It may even be possible to work on a military project by using advisors who handle all the sensitive information and parcel out what the rest of the team needs to know. However, the process of obtaining a security clearance isn't a daunting one. Even so, it always helps to be prepared.

Security Clearances

For the U.S., a person requires a security clearance if he or she will be in a position that will have or requires access to classified information. According to the U.S. Department of State's Web page, a security clearance is "a determination that a person is able and willing to safeguard classified national security information . . . based on his or her loyalty, character, trustworthiness, and reliability." There are three primary levels of security clearance: Confidential, Secret, and Top Secret. The different branches of the military as well as different government departments and agencies also have additional, highly specialized clearances above and beyond Top Secret.

Military personnel often have at least a Secret level clearance, and ex-military personnel may have an easier time getting security clearances. In most cases, the military sponsor will make the determination whether or not a security clearance will be needed for a developer on a project. It would be highly unusual for a developer to pre-emptively contact the U.S. Department of State and request a security clearance. However, you can certainly prepare yourself for an expected security screening by gathering the following information:

- List all the addresses you have lived at for the last 10 years.

- Names, phone numbers, and addresses of personal references at each of those addresses.

- Names, phone numbers, and addresses of all your employers in the last 10 years.

- List every trip overseas you have made throughout your life.

- List all relatives who are foreign nationals or who live in other countries.

- Make sure each person to be nominated for a security clearance has done this as well.

Other items of interest in the security clearance process are an arrest record (if any), drug use (if any), and so on. In general, says Jason Robar, founder of the consultancy AISA Group, "If you think it might be important, it probably is." So be as thorough as you can.

If your company or team contains foreign nationals, depending on where they are from, you might have issues in getting clearance. While getting clearance for foreign nationals isn't impossible, it can make your approval process take longer. Similarly, if you regularly outsource development, especially to companies in other nations, you should be aware that such outsourcing could be considered a security risk. At the very least, the security check may take longer because the outsourcing companies need to be checked as well.

Other countries, particularly those that use American military equipment, may be interested in the same software products as the U.S. military. Each country has its own process of security screening, but the information above would prove useful in these instances as well. U.S. citizens can certainly obtain security clearances in other countries.

Of course, not all military contracts involve sensitive information or require a security clearance. There are a multitude of other training tasks that the military would find useful. When asked about their most recent serious game project (see survey result 4.1), a minority of the serious game developers, sponsors, and researchers surveyed needed a security clearance to work on the game.

Serious Games Survey Result 4.1

Question: *Did you need a security clearance to work on your most recent serious game project?*

85.96%	No
14.04%	Yes

Question: *If yes, what level?*

25.00%	Confidential
50.00%	Secret
25.00%	Top Secret

(Survey Note: 57 Respondents)

Technology Re-Use Issues

There are several different development cases. In the first case, as a contractor or subcontractor for the military you are working on a project that is to be used exclusively by the military. Security will be much tighter in this case. Also, opportunities to leverage the work done on one project will almost certainly require that you pursue another military project, since your company may find that its intellectual property has been deemed Top Secret: You still own it, but the govern-ment has a say in how you can market it.

Full Spectrum Warrior, developed by Pandemic Studios in conjunction with ICT, cost about $6 million to develop and is an example of a game that was created for military training but that was also released in a modified version for the public.

In another case, you are working on a project for which the military sees potential military-specific applications. Contract work for the Department of Defense (DoD) as a part of the Small Business Innovation Research (SBIR) program is often of this sort. We will discuss SBIRs later in this chapter.

Developing for the Military

The military is anything but a homogenous organization, and there are many ways to work for the military. The military includes combat troops, of course, but there is also a vast infrastructure that trains and supplies the front line troops. While the huge military-industrial corporations like Raytheon Company and Lockheed Martin Corporation get most of the attention, they are not the only ones. Contractors and subcontractors to the military are many and varied.

New Development Case Study—BreakAway Games

BreakAway Games, a subsidiary of BreakAway Ltd. in Hunt Valley, MD, developed a computerized version of *Peloponnesian War* in the late 1990s for the National Defense University. A pen-and-paper version of *Peloponnesian War* had been in use for a number of years as part of the standard curriculum of certain military strategy courses. The Peloponnesian War is an excellent historical example of many strategic principles that have been studied to gain insight into the First World War, the Cold War, and, more recently, the Iraq War. The transition of the game from pen-and-paper to video game enhanced many aspects of the game, particularly the addition of multi-player features, and enriched the overall training experience. Unlike the Online Alchemy project discussed later in this chapter, BreakAway developed *Peloponnesian War* much like a commercial game project.

Deborah Tillett, President of BreakAway Ltd., said that working for the military, or other government agency, is not that different from working for a retail publisher. In both cases, you have to understand the market you're targeting, understand the organization you're working for, and know who it is in the organization that is ultimately responsible for approving projects. And, just like retail development, Tillett said, "everybody tries to committee you" and dictate how you should design and develop the game.

In order for a game developer to be attractive for these types of projects, Tillett said, they have to maintain their commercial presence. If they switch exclusively to military projects, or to government projects, the developer loses its value.

FIGURE 4.6

The Peloponnesian War

© BreakAway Games. Used with Permission

Mike McShaffry, Head of Studio for BreakAway Games in Austin, TX, pointed out a big difference in getting contracts in this arena. Unlike in the retail sector, if a developer lands a government contract that approval may be appealed. There is a mandatory waiting period where other companies who also bid on the contract can appeal. The government has to follow these rules for awarding contracts, though it may seem very odd—and very frustrating—to a developer whose experience has been wholly retail up to this point.

Another difference, McShaffry pointed out, is that the military is less interested in how the completed project *looks* and much more interested in how it *acts*. A simulation that is "good enough" for a retail game might fall very short of the specification demanded of a military-grade simulation. The military sets precise specifications for the behavior of certain aspects of the simulation, and it will not be satisfied unless those specifications are met or exceeded.

Modifying Existing Game Case Study—CogniToy

Beyond creating new, specialized games, the military is also open to using and adapting existing games. In 1999, CogniToy, an independent game developer in Boston, Massachusetts, released *MindRover: The Europa Project*. The game, a distant descendent of the classic *CRobots*, is about designing and programming robotic vehicles, and then letting them run loose and compete against other robots on Europa, a moon of Jupiter.

A feature of *MindRover* was a simulation of Lego Robotics. *MindRover*'s support of Lego Robotics extended to the ability to download the programs into vehicles constructed with Lego Robotics. "They would run around on the floor," Kent Quirk, CEO and owner of CogniToy, said, "and chase the cat."

In 2000, Accenture, working under a contract for the Defense Acquisition University (DAU), contacted Quirk about adapting *MindRover* to use in a course at DAU. The students of the DAU go on to become government purchasing agents. Or, as Quirk put it, the DAU trains "people who buy tanks and planes."

FIGURE 4.7

MindRover: The Europa Project

© CogniToy.
Used with Permission

The normal process for purchasing new equipment is for purchasers to fill out a Request for Proposal (RFP), outlining what is desired. Suppliers then write responses to the RFP, and the purchaser must evaluate the responses and choose the one that best meets the requirements for the best price. In one module of the DAU's training program, however, "the tables are turned" on the students. In this module, the students are given an RFP and must meet the specifications laid out in the RFP using the supplied materials.

Originally, this course used rubber bands and cardboard, but in the late 1990s had moved to using the Lego Robotics Invention System. Though an obvious improvement over the prior method, the logistics of managing the Lego bricks (where different colors represented different materials) and batteries proved to be a headache. Accenture suggested moving the process into the virtual realm, and the Lego Robotics simulation built in to *MindRover* seemed an obvious way to do it.

For the first year, in a single test class, CogniToy emulated within *MindRover* exactly what the DAU had been doing with Lego Robotics. In the years since then, through two additional contracts, CogniToy has worked with the DAU to make the class "less Lego, more realistic." After the first year, the contractor that CogniToy worked with shifted from Accenture to CSC. CogniToy is now further subcontracting the work on *MindRover* to another game developer.

The shift to the virtual realm has expanded the choices and challenges of the class. With the Lego Robotics, the students built remote controlled robots that moved over a carpet and fired a rubber-tipped missile at a stationary target. In *MindRover*, though, Quirk said, "we were able to change that to being in a city, with a target that doesn't sit still and could fire back. It's a much more realistic challenge."

Though most of the instructors were excited by the possibilities represented by the shift from the real world to the virtual world of *MindRover*, some resisted. Not only did the change require trusting a simulation and learning how to use new software, the student teams had to be reorganized around the new processes. "Now," Quirk said, "they've come to understand, as they work with more and more game-like technology, that learning is fun."

One of the best things about being a subcontractor versus a regular contractor, Quirk pointed out, was that the amount of paperwork required was much less. "There is no comparison to the game industry," he said about the paperwork CogniToy had to submit. He added, "You have to have a high tolerance for bureaucracy." Quirk recommended hiring someone who "enjoys" that kind of paperwork.

Quirk also stressed the need to be patient with the payment processing. The checks won't be released until the work is done and accepted, so you must be able to carry a bit of time on your payroll. "You have to do it the way they want it done," he said, "because you're not going to convince them that you have a better idea."

The Small Business Innovation Research (SBIR) Program

Perhaps the easiest way to get involved with developing for the military, and a number of other government agencies, is through the Small Business Innovation Research (SBIR) program.

Created in 1982, the SBIR program currently provides $1.6 billion each year to support research and development (R&D) for small businesses across the United States. In short, SBIR makes it possible for smaller companies (those with 500 or fewer employees) to participate in government research grants. SBIR projects cover many topics, including key technologies, and even some high-risk areas. The Department of Defense SBIR awards in 2003 came to almost $900 million.

SBIR Agencies

There are 11 agencies required by SBIR to reserve a portion of their R&D funds for awarding to small business:

- Department of Agriculture
- Department of Commerce
- Department of Defense
- Department of Education

- Department of Energy

- Department of Health and Human Services

- Department of Homeland Security

- Department of Transportation

- Environmental Protection Agency

- National Aeronautics and Space Administration

- National Science Foundation

Within the Department of Defense, the Air Force, Army, and Navy participate in the SBIR program, as well as the DARPA and the Missile Defense Agency.

According to the U.S. Small Business Administration's Web site (www.sba.gov), the following qualifications are required to participate in the SBIR program:

- The company is American-owned and independently operated.

- The company is a for-profit enterprise.

- The principal researcher for the project is employed by the company.

- The company has no more than 500 employees.

SBIRs happen in three phases. Phase I is the startup phase, with awards of up to $100,000. This phase is for exploring the technical merit and feasibility of the proposed idea or technology. The award is paid in installments: half at the halfway report and the remainder on completion of the final report. Phase I is generally a short timeframe, six months or less.

Phase II has awards up to $750,000 and has a longer timeframe. Phase II projects can take up to two years. A key goal of Phase II is the commercialization of the idea or technology. Only Phase I award winners can participate in Phase II of the SBIR.

The final phase, Phase III, takes the Phase II innovation from the laboratory and into the market. There are no SBIR funds for Phase III. Companies working on Phase III SBIR projects must secure private funding from other investors or get government funding from a different program.

SBIR Web Pages of Participating Agencies

Department of Agriculture (USDA) SBIR
www.csrees.usda.gov/funding/sbir/sbir.html

Department of Commerce (DOC)
DOC National Oceanic and Atmospheric Administration (NOAA)
SBIR/ORTA Page
www.ofa.noaa.gov/~amd/sbirs/sbir.html

DOC National Institute of Standards & Technology (NIST) SBIR Site
http://patapsco.nist.gov/ts_sbir/

Department of Defense (DoD)
www.acq.osd.mil/sadbu/sbir/

Air Force SBIR/STTR
www.afrl.af.mil/sbir/index.htm

Army SBIR/STTR
www.aro.army.mil/arowash/rt/sbir/sbir.htm

Navy SBIR/STTR
www.navysbir.com/

DARPA Small Business Center
www.darpa.mil/sbir/

DoD Special Operations Command
http://soal.socom.mil/index.cfm?page=sadbu&sb=sbir

Missile Defense Agency (MDA) SBIR Site
www.winbmdo.com/

Department of Education
www.ed.gov/programs/sbir/index.html

Department of Energy
http://sbir.er.doe.gov/sbir/

Department of Health and Human Services
National Institutes of Health (NIH)
http://grants.nih.gov/grants/funding/sbir.htm

Department of Homeland Security
www.hsarpasbir.com/

Department of Transportation
www.volpe.dot.gov/sbir/

Reasons why you would be interested in the SBIR program:

- It's *grant* money, not a loan, so you don't have to pay it back.

- You do not give up ownership or equity in your project or company.

- SBIR projects are connected to real-world problems in a wide variety of subject areas.

There are many rules and regulations for participating in the SBIR program beyond being a qualifying business, as listed earlier. There are specific submission formats, and each of the participating departments has its own requirements. The following case study touches on some of those issues.

SBIR Case Study—Online Alchemy

Originally founded to create a new type of game engine, the Dynemotion engine, Online Alchemy, an independent game developer in Austin, TX, found that its efforts were of interest to DARPA. Specifically, DARPA expressed an interest in Online Alchemy's work on creating more realistic non-player character (NPC) behavior. Though already working on a commercial game to showcase the Dynemotion engine, the work for the SBIR "dovetailed nicely" with Online Alchemy's efforts and business plan, said Craig Fryar, VP of Online Alchemy. At the time of the interview for this book, Online Alchemy had sent in the last paperwork to complete Phase I of the SBIR.

"When we first looked at SBIR it was daunting," Fryar said. The specification for the project had a broad scope, much broader than any one company could manage. Fryar suspected that the sponsor of the SBIR was trying to "test the mettle" of the companies that responded. Not all SBIRs are like that.

One of the challenges Online Alchemy faced in Phase I was condensing their proposal to the 25-page format (which means *exactly* 25 pages) required for the SBIR. For people with an engineering background, Fryar pointed out, it can be difficult to fully describe an idea in such a limited space. You have to describe the team, the statement of work, the required resources, and so on, in addition to the actual technology you're proposing and make sure it follows a specific format. Less like a business plan than a technical design specification, the Phase I proposal includes less marketing and financial information and more engineering. The SBIR called for some deviations from the company's game concept, but addressing those deviations, Fryar said, should improve the completed game.

According to Fryar, the government gets a royalty-free license to use the technology developed in the course of the SBIR. Despite this, the ownership of the technology (and the patent on that technology) remains with Online Alchemy. In other words, the U.S. government is providing funding to help Online Alchemy develop its technology in exchange for the right to use it any way the government sees fit.

When the project is completed, Online Alchemy is permitted, and is in fact *expected*, to use the technology they developed in its own commercial endeavors. It can be used in games or in licensed products created for other purposes. This kind of commercial development is a key part of the SBIR process. The government wants to see ongoing commercial development. In short, Fryar said, "We've received additional funding to help us do what we were doing anyway."

With the time it takes to be accepted for the SBIR, and with award money from the SBIRs coming in installments, game developers interested in pursuing the SBIR program will need to have sufficient funding to carry them for a number of months. It is very important to set aside some money to cover payroll and other expenses in the opening months. This is true of most grant funding programs, not just the military, as we will see in other chapters.

Fryar offers the following advice to developers who are interested in SBIR projects:

- Don't assume your idea for or response to the SBIR is unique. Do your research, possibly including patent searches, and be open to criticism. On the other hand, he said, don't compromise your project (by exposing it to the public or by changing your project to better match the SBIR) just to get the award money.

- Take the time to be certain you understand the intent of the SBIR and its sponsor. If you don't understand the purpose of the SBIR, you could be wasting valuable time and resources.

- Surround yourself with people who have done SBIRs and ask for their advice and feedback. The SBIR Phase I report format is very specific, and having the assistance of someone who has done it before can prove invaluable. Also, there are SBIR-specific dates for submissions and when you can and can't talk with the SBIR sponsor, as well as other possible pitfalls that can trap the SBIR rookie.

- Don't get discouraged. The number of companies who get approved for SBIRs the first time is very small (less than 10 percent). If you want to participate in the SBIR program, you need to learn the process and keep trying.

Further advice for SBIR hopefuls is

- Get help from the SBIR sponsor, though be aware of when you can and can't discuss the SBIR with him or her.

- Don't try to be the answer to the whole SBIR. Focus on what you can do best. SBIR awards are not exclusive. Multiple contracts can be awarded.

- Check in with the SBIR Regional Officer for more information.

In certain cases, if a sponsor is very impressed by your ongoing work or if you propose work on a related topic, the sponsor may even write a customized SBIR for you.

In the world of military contracting, SBIRs are just one possibility. In fact, SBIRs are quite small compared to the huge contracts awarded to the likes of Boeing Company or Northrop Grumman Corporation. However, SBIRs represent a viable first step for newcomers to military contracting, and the contacts gained during the SBIR process may prove invaluable later.

The Small Business Technology Transfer (STTR) Program

The STTR program is the companion to the SBIR program. The STTR program, created in 1992, is smaller than the SBIR program (2003 DoD STTR awards came to just under $50 million). The qualifications for the STTR program, however, are similar to those of the SBIR program:

- The company is American-owned and independently operated.

- The company is a for-profit enterprise.

- The principal researcher for the project is employed by the company.

- The company has no more than 500 employees.

- A U.S.-based research institute must be involved.

To date, the STTR program has been less known than the SBIR program for serious games. This is probably due to the research institute involvement requirement and the overall smaller profile of the STTR program.

PITCHING TO THE MILITARY

Besides the SBIR program or other RFP-based programs, there is another way to land military contracts. Even if you don't have a fully appropriate existing (or near-existing) product at the right time, the military, like retail game publishers, is receptive to good ideas. Just as in the retail arena, when pitching to the military, you have to be able to show them how your idea helps *them*.

The easiest way to approach the military is to arrange presentations for representatives of the various services at conferences, like the Interservice/Industry Training, Simulation and Education Conference (I/ITSEC), Serious Games Summit (especially when the conference is held in Washington, D.C.), or the G.A.M.E.S. Synergy Summit. There are often representatives of the various military divisions at these conferences. If the agency you're interested in has a booth, then that would be an easy way to get the necessary contact information. This is analogous to approaching publishers at the Game Developers Conference (GDC) or Electronic Entertainment Expo (E3).

In a pitch, you should always focus on the customer. You become a topic of the discussion only insofar as you can show how you can help them get what they want. This doesn't change, regardless of the target industry.

In his article, "Getting Serious About New Opportunities," Ben Sawyer offers the following "talking points" when pitching serious games:

- "Games are simulations too."

- The current generation has a lot of experience playing games.

- "Learning is inherent in games."

- Games improve the odds that people will learn (play) on their own.

- Games provide a way to measure everything a player does.

- Games can be a powerful alternative to other teaching methods.

There are many in the military who still need to be convinced as to the efficacy or wisdom of entrusting warfighter training to video games. As Clive Thompson pointed out in his August 2004 *New York Times* article, *The Making of an XBox Warrior*, "Army culture is deeply physical: Training is about sweating hard and keeping your boots in the mud. Video games, in that context, can seem like a frivolous or even dangerous detour from real-world experience." The above talking points seek to get past the skeptics by leveraging the similarity of games to existing simulations used for training, the proven strength of games in getting and keeping the attention of players, and the game developer's experience in making video games.

CONCLUSION

The military has a long history of using games and simulations to teach strategy and tactics. The U.S. military has for years been one of the biggest, if not *the* biggest, source of funding for training and simulation development. As the need for training continues to grow, and the tools and techniques for training become more widespread and better known, their level of investment is only going to grow.

Outside the United States, military organizations around the globe are also looking to use serious games to train their troops and prepare themselves for war in the 21st Century.

The future is always built with the tools and techniques being researched and created today. Advances in cognitive and emotional modeling will allow serious games to better simulate reality beyond simple physics, providing almost-real interaction possibilities. Fully immersive virtual reality may still be a long way into the future, but serious games don't have to operate at that level to be effective.

In the next chapter, we'll look at the rest of the government sector and how other agencies are using serious games.

CHAPTER

GOVERNMENT GAMES

When most people think of doing work for the government, they tend to think of doing that work for the national government, and for the military in particular. However, the government is much bigger than just the military, and governing happens on a variety of levels:

- National

- State (or provincial)

- County (or parish or shire)

- Municipality (city, town, or village)

The greatest funding is at the national level, of course, but state or provincial governments and even municipal governments all have training needs, information they wish to pass on to the public, and taxpayer funding.

In this chapter, we will focus on those areas of government outside the military (which was covered in Chapter 4) that have developed or shown an interest in serious games. We will review some of the past efforts of government entities in creating serious games and take a look at some of the current projects coming out and underway. Finally, we will discuss the more technical aspects of developing for the government.

Survey of Government Games

As we've already mentioned, government agencies aren't limited to the national level. Many countries are divided up into states or provinces, which have smaller agencies to oversee those areas. Those states may even join forces for regional approaches. At the more local level, there are the county and city governments, which have agencies of their own. At each level, the available pool of taxpayer money gets smaller, but the projects also become more personal and more significant to the interested agencies.

On the other side of the spectrum, there is the possibility of countries working together in the spirit of international cooperation, such as in the case of tsunami relief or other disasters. Countries may want to band together to perform analyses on proposed policies that would affect many nations like free trading alliances or global warming restrictions. With increasing globalization, the policy decisions of one government can have repercussions throughout the world.

National Agencies

According to Clark Abt in his book, *Serious Games*, the government, like industry, is interested in analyzing and solving specific, concrete problems. In the situations where serious games can help government agencies solve such problems, they have already generated some interest and activity. The U.S. government in particular has shown a willingness to experiment with video games as training tools. According to Jason Robar of the AISA Group, "Just about every level of the U.S. government is realizing that modeling and simulation is important. The military has led the efforts, but other agencies are looking into it as well."

First Responders and Black Swans

Training and simulation within the government can encompass a broad range of activities, from ethics training to firefighting. As is evident from Chapter 4 on the military, training can be highly effective in preparing for situations of immense stress, which should prove useful to first responders of any kind as well as counter-terrorist and intelligence agencies. Already, the Secret Service has used the *America's Army* platform to stage mission rehearsals. In emergency situations, it is imperative that disparate government agencies coordinate their efforts toward the same goal. Thus simulations used in the government can go way beyond mere weapons and equipment training.

"Black swan" is a phrase that has come into more common usage since the events of September 11, 2001. In his April 8, 2004, *New York Times* editorial, Nassim Taleb defined a black swan as "an outlier, an event that lies beyond the realm of normal expectations." Without wading into the article's debate of whether or not 9/11 represents a black swan, the concept of a black swan is that it's an unpredictable event that defies prediction. In other words, it's an anomalous occurrence. Preparing for this black swan has been the thrust of many efforts by the Department of Homeland Security (DHS) and other federal agencies. When that black swan occurs, it's hoped that simulations will help people get past the shock of the unexpected and be mentally prepared to take action.

For this purpose, the FBI has used simulations like *Angel Five*, developed by Visual Purple, to train its agents in crisis management. *Angel Five* models a WMD terrorist attack, and the trainee must coordinate resources between federal, state, and local agencies. Similarly, BreakAway Games' *Incident Commander*, funded by the Department of Justice, trains first responders and federal employees in the new National Incident Management System, which standardizes response methods for dealing with terrorist attacks or natural disasters. In late 2004 the Transportation Security Administration, along with UNITECH, a company with experience in multimedia training, began work on simulations for training security personnel at U.S. seaports. Visual Purple also created *Dangerous Contract* for the USDA to train its administrators to deal with an infectious disease outbreak.

It's clear that the government has faith in the training power of simulations. Beginning in 2004, DHS is allowing local authorities to purchase video games and other simulations with federal grant money, provided they consult the department's guidelines. DHS is comprised of 22 disparate agencies, from the Coast Guard to the Secret Service, and its responsibilities include customs, border protection, transportation security, preparedness and disaster recovery, infrastructure protection, and cyber security as well as research and development in science and technology that assists those responsibilities.

This could hold a lot of opportunities for game developers. In addition to training simulations, such as those for pilots and vessel operators to learn radar and navigational equipment, DHS funds emergency response simulations. It has conducted large-scale disaster preparedness exercises with dummy victims in cities across the United States, but these live-action exercises tie up personnel and equipment and open up the possibility of litigation, and even panic, in the citizenry.

A key advantage of computer simulations is that emergency scenarios can be run over and over, with variations in severity and locations and more, at little extra cost in manpower and material resources. This kind of repeated practice in extreme circumstances is hard to duplicate in the real world. In the virtual world of the computer, though, another major emergency is only a mouse click away.

These types of simulations allow first responders like the police, fire fighters, and emergency medicine technicians practice handling events and disasters that are expensive or even impossible to attempt in the real world. Simulations like the *3D Wild Land Fire Simulation* discussed in the "Fire Fighter Training" case study below save money and lives.

First responders aren't the only ones in the government who need to consider black swans. Games have even helped shape national policy, though often in only subtle ways. Richard Clarke, the former American counter-terrorism chief, said the following in an interview with Frank Rich for his January 6, 2005, *New York Times* article, "We'll Win This War—on '24'": "In both the Clinton and Bush administrations, the only time I was really effective in getting senior officers to pay attention was when I had tabletop war games." He added, "That did more than any briefing paper I might write."

Public Policy, Ethics Training, and More

Many believe simulations have the power to influence public policy. For this reason, the Markle Foundation, a not-for-profit organization, funded the development of *SimHealth* in the mid-1990s. Developed by Thinking Tools, a company spun off from Maxis (now owned by Electronic Arts), in *SimHealth* the player is a politician making policy decisions about health care. Although *SimHealth* was not developed specifically by a government agency, the game was used by the White House, politicians, insurers, academics, consultants, and the general public during that period to get a better understanding of the issues involved. After the Clinton administration abandoned the health care reform issue, interest in the game disappeared. During that same period, Maxis also promoted its *SimCity* title as a tool of city planners.

Games, particularly strategy games, can give players a chance to reflect upon their actions. In this way, they are particularly useful to portray the consequences of player decisions. While policymaking or military strategy is an obvious fit, games can even be used to promote ethics. In the 1990s, the Department of Justice spent $250,000 over four years to build a DOS-based game, *Quandaries*, as an ethics training tool. According to the DOJ's Web page, *Quandaries* was designed to teach federal employees how to apply the Standards of Conduct. In the game, the player starts at the entry level in a federal job. To be promoted in the game, the player must demonstrate knowledge of federal ethics rules.

Furthermore, simulations are widely accepted as useful tools to model scientific behavior. NASA, who produced the first computer-generated images as part of its Apollo Program in the 1960s, continues to rely heavily on that technology. For instance, in the 1990s, the *Distributed Earth Model and Orbiter Simulation* (DEMOS) was developed at NASA's Johnson Space Center initially as a mission planning and visualization tool. Later expanded and modified, it provided ground crews with a 3D depiction of what was happening on a space mission.

Similarly, the Federal Aviation Administration (FAA) created advanced simulations to model air traffic patterns at airports and used them to train air traffic controllers. To train marine pilots, the Maritime Administration built a full-scale simulator designed to mimic a ship's bridge, with a computer-generated projection of actual ports and waterways around the world.

pullUin software provides an example of the possible variety of government funded projects. Since the company was founded in 2000, pullUin software has worked with a number of government agencies, creating specialized games and game-like products. With the United Stated Department of Agriculture, the company created *Care Connections*, a training program to address the lecture-based requirements for Nursing Assistant certifications. And with a grant from the Department of Education, the company developed *Creature Control: the Quest for Homeostasis* to teach middle school science students about homeostasis.

As of this writing, the Federal Emergency Management Agency (FEMA) has a section of its Web page set aside for children, called "FEMA for KIDS." Containing a collection of interactive Web pages, including simple games, stories, coloring books, and more, FEMA for KIDS teaches "how to be prepared for disasters and prevent disaster damage." Even the Bureau of Engraving and Printing, which prints Federal Reserve Notes (money), now includes a section on its Web page with small games for children, ostensibly teaching currency authentication (how to spot counterfeits).

International

Other nations have also begun using video games to train personnel. Kevin Corti of PIXELearning in the United Kingdom, talked about opportunities in the European Union (EU). "One of the benefits of the European Union for private companies," he said, "is that they can bid for funds on a varying scale through a multitude of funding instruments that the EU uses to address key priority areas." Such priority areas include "everything from skills to nanotechnology." The Community Research and Development Information Service (CORDIS) is the gateway to these instruments. PIXELearning is one of several companies that have had games-based learning work funded by the EU.

VStep, based in Rotterdam, Netherlands, in the European Union, has created a number of training games, including *Port of Rotterdam Incident Configurator*, *Fire Brigade Commander Training*, and *Company Safety Officer Training*. And in France, developers have created a game for the French Civilian Defense to train fire fighters at all levels in forest fire techniques.

In Japan, at the Disaster Social Engineering Laboratory at Gunma University in Kiryu Gunma, developers created the *OWASE Dynamic Tsunami Hazard Map*. This Web-based application forecasts loss of life from tsunami events. The simulation estimates the number of casualties based on parameters set by the user, with variables for levels of preparation and response time of emergency management, citizens, and local infrastructure. According to the *OWASE* Web page, the "influence of various response scenarios on the number of casualties clearly illustrates the relationship between tsunami hazard preparation and disaster prevention."

In 2005, the United Nations World Food Programme (WFP), headquartered in Rome, Italy, released its first online game, *Food Force*. The game was developed for the PC and Mac by European game developers Deepend and Playerthree, and is available for free. The goal of *Food Force* is to raise awareness about global hunger. In the game, players get points by air-dropping food rations and surveying war-torn populations on the fictitious island of Sheylan.

Case Study—Fire Fighter Training

Dynamic Animation Systems (DAS) has been designing and building virtual reality applications for entertainment, education, and the government, including the military, since 1995. DAS specializes in using its own core game technology and using it to quickly create contracted projects.

In 2000, the National Fire Academy (NFA) contracted DAS to build a computer based simulation and training network. The result was the *National Fire Academy Training Simulation*, a LAN networked simulation that allows instructors to present a variety of fire fighting situations to their students. The students interact with the simulation over the network, sending their response plans to the instructor.

After deploying the *National Fire Academy Training Simulation*, the United States Department of Agriculture (USDA) Forest Service, which had similar fire fighting training needs, contracted with DAS to extend that application. The result was the *3D Wild Land Fire Simulation*, a wild fire simulation with physically realistic fire propagation.

In both cases, according to Russell Bowers, Program Manager for FEMA projects at DAS, the training was less about the specific tools and techniques of fire fighting and more about instilling "recognition prime decision making," or RPD.

RPD is a model for how experts make decisions under stressful situations. The students rely on their training and experience to quickly assess the situation facing them and attempt to come up with an acceptable course of action. Their plan is then played out in the simulation to see whether or not it needs to be modified. If their first plan proves to be ineffective, they can go back, select another option, and run through the simulation again.

Because of the emphasis on RPD, the assessment needs of the simulation are pretty straightforward. In short, the instructor can take the trainee's response and let it play out in the simulation. If the response works, or has a favorable result, then it is considered acceptable. If not, then the trainee tries again. The goal is for the trainee to have an almost subconscious ability to see the situation, understand it, immediately eliminate unsuitable options, and then pick from the much smaller selection of acceptable solutions. This skill is almost always the result of the experience from facing a number of situations. The simulation makes it possible to face any number of such situations without having to burn a single tree or risk any lives.

There is no built-in test and no tracking of metrics to compute a numerical score, said Aaron Greb, Senior Programmer on the project. Instead, the simulations are designed so that the instructors can create scenarios with certain elements in mind (see Figure 5.1). By reviewing how the students respond to the scenarios, the instructor can assess their understanding of those elements.

Unlike the fire propagation models used in some retail fire fighting games, said Greb, the *3D Wild Land Fire Simulation* strove to be as accurate as possible, basing the fire's growth and propagation on available fuel types in the chosen terrain, a variety of environmental conditions, and even the terrain's topology. Trainees can request resources and build fire lines to hinder and stop fire spreading. At the same time, instructors can alter the environmental conditions and affect the behavior of the fire.

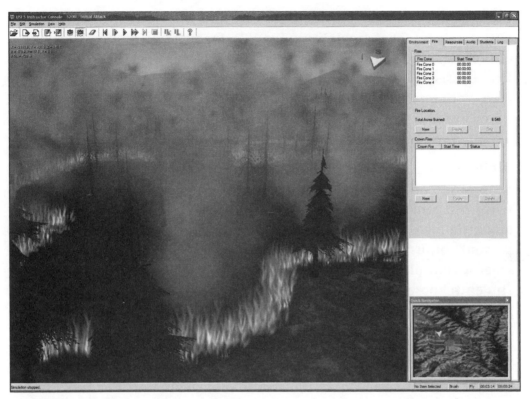

FIGURE 5.1

3D Wild Land Fire Simulation Instructor Station

© DAS. Used with Permission

Like CogniToy and *MindRover*, discussed in Chapter 4, DAS has received additional contracts to add new features and incorporate new simulation effects each year. As the Forest Service's use of the product evolves and its understanding of what's possible with the simulation expands, DAS has been asked to add on more functionality. "They weren't positive exactly what they wanted at first," Bowers said. Therefore, the simulations had to be developed from scratch, and then customized as the instructors discovered what they needed.

A big difference between creating games for entertainment versus simulations of this type for the government, Greb said, is that the scope of government projects tends to be very specific. Government agencies, including the military, have a very specific goal in mind. They want software created with a narrow list of capabilities. The NFA, for example, wanted a collection of precreated scenarios, such as fires in school buildings and churches and fires caused by chemical spills. The Forest Service wanted to display rural areas with trees and be able to burn them. The story elements, the dynamic nature of the game play, and larger scope of retail video games is not expected or desired.

While the simulations have some elements close to the retail genre of real-time strategy (RTS) games, there is none of the "eye candy" often associated with such games. For instance, the *3D Wild Land Fire Simulation* doesn't show any little men or any firefighting equipment. This was deliberate so as to prevent confusion in the trainees whose local resources might not match what was displayed. "All you see is a fire spreading," Greb said. When the student chooses to create a fire line or a dig a trench, those are simply added, with no unnecessary animation.

State or Provincial Agencies

Many states have agencies that are similar to the national or federal agencies but with a more local focus. The state agencies may also have different structures, goals, and emphases. As Tip O'Neill observed so long ago, "All politics is local."

In the United States, as an example, Native American issues are overseen at the national level by the Bureau of Indian Affairs, which is a part of the Department of the Interior. Many of the 50 states, however, also have their own agencies that handle Native American issues within the state. In Oklahoma, that is the Native American Services agency for the Oklahoma Nations and Tribes.

An early example of a game used at the state or regional level is *Corridor*, a computer-assisted human-player simulation game that explored the political and economic factors in the formulation and implementation of regional transportation policy. *Corridor* modeled the Northeast Corridor, from Boston to Washington D.C., dividing the territory into nodes, or major urban centers. Players could play a federal official, a state official, a transportation industry representative, or a representative of transportation consumers.

Some states have already begun using serious games to highlight the tough decisions faced by politicians and policy makers. In 2003, students at the Worcester Polytechnic Institute in Massachusetts created *MassBalance*, a Web-based simulation of the 2004 Massachusetts state budget. Though *MassBalance* presented a highly simplified version of the state budget, it preserved enough complexity to show how difficult it can be to allocate funds at the state level, spreading limited funds across necessary services and infrastructure maintenance while also seeking new development and desirable social services.

Hazmat: Hotzone is a game being produced by a graduate student at Entertainment Technology Center (ETC) at Carnegie Mellon University in Pittsburgh, Pennsylvania. Built in collaboration with the Fire Department of New York and built with video game technology, *Hazmat: Hotzone* is intended to be an "instructor-based simulation" for training first responders in handling hazardous materials emergencies with an emphasis on "awareness, teamwork, and decision-making skills." Like *Peacemaker*, another ETC project discussed in Chapter 9, *Hazmat: Hotzone* is still in development as of this writing.

Other aspects of state governance that have used serious games or game-like simulations include hunter education certification, driver education, boat operation and safety education, and more. The defensive driving courses sometimes required because of speeding tickets have used driving games. Each of these types of certification varies state by state, but the information can be found with a minimum of research.

The federal government sometimes assists in promoting state-level development. In 2004, for example, the Department of Homeland Security asked for $5 million to create the Rural Domestic Preparedness Consortium, which would take a regional approach to training first responders. This would allow the state programs to be customized for the different needs of the different states. Some states, like Texas, have border control issues, while others, like Oregon, have seaports.

State-Level Case Study—
Caltrans Project Management Simulation

When the California Department of Transportation (Caltrans) changed its project management structure and procedures, putting engineers into much closer proximity to the project managers, the officials there wanted a training tool to help the two groups better understand each other. Caltrans wanted the game to teach engineers about the role of project managers and their duties and responsibilities. In short, Caltrans wanted a tool to teach project management to non-project managers, said Clark Quinn, founder of Quinnovation and author of the recent book, *Engaging Learning: Designing e-Learning Simulation Games*.

In *The Caltrans Project Management Simulation*, the player is Durka, an alien who is the new project manager for planet terraforming. Durka's job is to get all of the terraforming projects completed on time, while maintaining good relations with his team and the various project stakeholders. One of the main challenges of the game is spotting incorrect data coming in, and then communicating with the appropriate team members to get the data corrected. The other big challenge of the game is communication with the team members and the project stakeholders. Different characters have different personalities and need to be approached and dealt with differently.

The light-hearted, science fiction motif of the game was deliberate, Quinn said. The exaggeration of the characters and the situations, as well as the simplifying and removal of non-necessary details, he went on, have proven to be powerful tools for both learning and for engagement. Though sometimes other clients, both in government and especially in the corporate space, prove resistant to this approach, Quinn added, Caltrans was open to the idea. Quinn had worked with Caltrans on an earlier, simpler project using some of the same characters and storyline elements, and that experience had helped Caltrans to take the leap from extreme realism into Durka's world.

The biggest challenges of the project, Quinn said, involved extracting the "real instructional objectives," or learning goals. For *The Caltrans Project Management Simulation*, beyond teaching the basics of project management, the team also wanted the game to promote better relations between project managers and engineers. The Caltrans team knew what it wanted in general terms, but it didn't understand how to frame the project's objectives as learning goals.

Quinn repeatedly stressed the importance of starting with the instructional objectives when designing a serious game. These objectives will lead the designer to the task or tasks that will then teach the player what he or she needs to learn. If you don't have people involved who understand learning, he said, the final product might look good and demonstrate strong production values, but ultimately it may not meet the necessary learning goals. Thus the design team has to understand both learning and engagement.

Quinn said *The Caltrans Project Management Simulation* bears some resemblance to strategy games in that the player is constantly checking on the status of various projects and making sure those projects get done on time. However, when designing the game, Quinn wasn't trying to fit the mold for any particular retail genre. He focused on creating a storyline that put decisions in front of the player that reinforced the desired learning goals.

DEVELOPING GOVERNMENT GAMES

Developing serious games for government agencies may seem to experienced game developers like a huge departure from their area of expertise. To new developers just getting started, publishers already seem daunting enough, and the government might appear impossible to approach. Even though there are many differences between government agencies and retail publishers, there are just as many similarities.

The design process for serious games is not radically different from the design of other video games. Of course, the shift in emphasis from fun to learning does have its impact. There is the reduced scope, as Greb and Bowers mentioned, and the need for increased accuracy in simulation. While it may appear that simulations are the rule, they are just one of many options.

In both cases, the developer is either pitching an original idea to a (hopefully) interested party or pitching to a proposal (bidding on a contract) that has been made by the interested party. The funding for the project is being provided by, or through, the interested party. And, in both cases, the developer should expect primary remuneration upfront, with little hope of ever seeing any money on the back end.

Designing

Game developers often begin the design process by first deciding on the genre of the game. Genre refers to whether the game is a first-person shooter (FPS), a real-time strategy game (RTS), a role-playing game (RPG), and so on. Deciding the genre of the game does offer some advantages. First, experienced players are familiar with established genres and recognize the set of conventions for user interface design, story elements, and so on. Secondly, and most importantly for the publishers, genres allow publishers a degree of control over their business plans and game release schedules.

Within the serious game space, though, the genre of the game is less important. The primary goals of the serious game are to educate, train, and inform. With government games, how retail stores would categorize a game is less important. Any genre of game can be used as long as the game achieves the desired goal or goals.

Just like there is latitude in genre in serious games designed for the government, there is also latitude in regards to subject matter. The multitude of departments and agencies that is any national government has an interest in a great many types of training. Beyond training for specific skills and emergency preparation, there is interest in training for leadership, teamwork, and similar concepts, and even in educating citizens in how their government works. Whether these games are simulations or more like traditional video games, the important thing is that the game provides the desired result.

Design Considerations

3D graphical simulations with detailed, real-world physics have been used for many government games, but even this semigenre is not required. In many cases, simulating the relationships between people, or between economic forces, or more, is more important than whether the game accurately portrays gravity. Of course, in serious games for NASA, gravity (or the lack of it) is very important. But in a game like *Quandaries*, which taught judgment and ethics, it has no place.

However, if the simulation concerns something like how a fire spreads or how other real-world physical or chemical processes function and react within their environments, then the developer will need to represent those processes as accurately possible. As we discussed in Chapter 3, designers often use a number of shortcuts that get the in-game simulation "close enough." These shortcuts will need to be carefully considered before they are applied so that they don't reduce the effectiveness of the simulation for training.

Many of the disaster preparedness programs are focused on coordinating roles and responsibilities across local, state, and federal organizations. Games designed in this arena should strive to accurately portray interagency dependencies as well as help to overcome obstacles to communication. The games shouldn't just be about how things are. With proper design, these games can help to create new policies and build the future of interagency cooperation.

As was discussed in the previous chapter, the artificial intelligence (AI) of non-player-characters (NPCs) in the games needs to be sufficient to accurately model the actions and responses of terrorists, citizens, and any other stand-ins. Government agencies have demonstrated a significant interest in this aspect of serious games. The Central Intelligence Agency, for example, has invested millions to develop a video game to teach its analysts to think like terrorists. In the same vein, Online Alchemy, as we discussed in Chapter 4, attracted the attention of DARPA with its work on generating more emotionally realistic NPCs.

An important design consideration that might be unexpected by game developers is support for people with disabilities. In the summer of 2001, the United States federal government implemented Section 508, an amendment to the Rehabilitation Act of 1973. Section 508 requires that the federal government acquire only electronic and information technology goods and services that provide for access by people with disabilities. As the Section 508 Web page (www.section508.gov) puts it, "Without the ability to hear what is being spoken, or to hear dialogue without the necessary visual context, these products can be confusing or useless to people with disabilities." This type of accessibility is also important in serious games for the corporate world, as we will discuss in Chapter 7.

Transparency of Design

Many serious games developed for government agencies can benefit from what is called "transparency of design." Transparency of design means that how the game simulation works is made available to interested players. This presentation of the internal logic and data used by the game opens the game up to modification and tinkering, and it is already a popular feature of many retail video games.

In some cases, this transparency and easy modification can result in free research being done by players, like curious students or dedicated researchers. For example, a simulation of a contentious topic like global warming could allow players to tweak the data used to drive the simulation. While this allows people to drive the simulation to produce their own predetermined idea of what the results should be, it also allows for easy updates and extensions, which improve the accuracy of the simulation. As new data becomes available, or as new interactions in data are discovered, the new information could be added.

The Element of Fun

How much fun should be designed into serious games is discussed several times in this book. Each market has a different take on how important fun is for its serious games. In the government market, there is a wide spectrum. Games for training first responders, for example, are going to be much more serious than those created to help children learn about the conservation of natural resources. The goals of the serious game have a strong influence on how the material is presented and how light-hearted or fun it should be.

Pitching

When pitching games to the government, one difference experienced game developers will notice is that they don't have to target their pitch for the publisher's marketing department. How the proposed game will fit into the publisher's plans for the upcoming fiscal year is just not an issue. Instead, the developer will be focusing on the needs of the policy maker or agency and demonstrating how the game will meet those needs.

The National Level

The United States government programs, such as the Small Business Innovation Research (SBIR), are a way for game developers to work with federal agencies, such as the Department of Agriculture, the Department of Education, and the Department of Defense. (The SBIR program is discussed in detail in Chapter 4.)

At the other end of the scale from the SBIR program are the Broad Agency Announcements (BAAs). Unlike SBIRs, which generally run in the $50,000 to $500,000 range with projects measured in months, BAA projects can have millions of dollars earmarked for funding projects that extend three to five years. SBIRs are also the domain of small companies (<500 employees) while BAAs often involve coalitions of companies, like Raytheon and Lockheed-Martin.

In the United States, whether the projects are for the military or any other government agency, the processes for getting the contract and the budget paperwork are similar. All government projects follow the same set of guidelines from the Office of Personnel Management (OPM).

Agencies and departments that don't have the necessary money in their budgets have to submit a budget request. The request must be for an identified need relevant to the agency. Without the need, Congress won't allocate any money in the next national budget. If the agency gets the money, then they will post Requests for Proposals (RFPs) and Requests for Information (RFIs) and award contracts to the winners.

Regarding DHS, its opportunities are listed at www.hsarpabaa.com and www.hsarpasbir.com. It regularly holds Vendor Outreach sessions for developers interested in networking and learning more about DHS. There is also a Mentor-Protégé Program that pairs up small companies with large companies. The smaller company would become a subcontractor for DHS.

Concerning opportunities in the EU, Corti pointed out that it's "important to realize that you can't get direct cash in the form of venture capital or for easily realizable product/service development." Developers would be working with partners like public organizations, such as chambers of commerce, research bodies and universities, and so on. Corti also said, "Whilst there is lots of money floating around, it takes forever to obtain (for example, a year), involves a huge amount of paperwork, is competitive, not overly transparent, and most funding is at a rate of a maximum of 50 percent of projects costs (and exclude any capital spending). You can also count on a big delay on getting the final payments." So while it may not be the best or fastest option for funding, it does exist, and interested developers will want to look into it.

State or Province Level

There is no one-stop-shop where developers can go and learn about all the opportunities available in all the states of the USA. As we discussed earlier, in the United States, each state has its own, unique structure and organization of government. This extends into the various agencies of the state government.

Even within a single state, it may take an actual visit to the state capital. Go to various agency offices and talk to people face to face to find out about available interest, funding, and projects. The state governments have their own Web sites, but the level of detail made available varies widely. Developers may need to have a team member on staff whose sole responsibility is to keep track of state and local issues, with an eye toward possible game-like projects.

Working for state agencies can be a very different experience from working for national government agencies. The bidding process is not standardized, as it is at the national level, and often the bidding process is limited to, or heavily weighted toward, companies based in the state. On the plus side, that "home field advantage," combined with proven expertise in game development, could help a developer get attention.

The budget for serious game projects at the state level will at times be smaller than budgets for similar project at the national level, but not always. Without the tax base of an entire nation to draw from, the pool of funds is significantly smaller. Projects will need to be scaled appropriately.

Local Level

The last half of the 20th century saw the growth of competition between large cities for the attention of corporations and government agencies. Cities that can convince a corporation to relocate its headquarters or to build a new factory or manufacturing plant within the city limits can reap a windfall for the local economy in the form of new taxes, new jobs, new growth, and more. For that reason, cities have poured more money than ever before into promoting the advantages of their location with business-friendly ordinances and amenities. Video games that can aid in that purpose would almost certainly attract attention and taxpayer-financed funding.

Like every other government entity, cities have the need to train their employees and their emergency service personnel. Indeed, in the wake of 9/11, New York City created its own intelligence units to assess threats to the area. Major metropolitan centers in the U.S. are following its example. While some broad-based training programs can be used, and though national programs cover some of it, there are always local differences that must be addressed.

Beyond the normal governing bodies, nearly every community in the U.S. and the rest of the modern world has an Arts and Humanities Council or local equivalent. Such councils have as their mission to promote local history, enhance local art and culture, and encourage participation in the local culture. Though the funding for such projects may not be large compared to retail projects, and possibly may be non-existent, there are other benefits:

- Increased local awareness of the developer.

- Increased local press coverage for the developer.

- Improved awareness about the developer, and game development issues, at the local government level.

Again, a developer would need to be aware of local issues and their champions and opponents to have the best chance of spotting and getting involved in those issues. For example, a local advocacy group may be interested in a simulation that shows how widening a popular street would not only increase traffic on the street, but also would have other, less desirable aspects. Among the issues would be higher vehicle speeds leading to more accidents, including accidents involving pedestrians, greater air and noise pollution, and so on. How would a developer even know about this kind of a project unless its employees lived in the area and kept up with the local civic and political news?

Developing for the Government

Besides having to deal with the alphabet soup of acronyms that seem to accompany every aspect of government, from DoD to SBIR to FEMA to BAA and on and on, there are other issues game developers should be aware of when working for the government. On the upside, at least the government doesn't care if you get the game finished in time for Christmas and isn't likely to force you to release it before it's ready.

The Internet and the Web have done wonders in connecting government agencies to each other and to the population at large. This has not, however, created a single standard for computer hardware and software. The government has no single specification for computer hardware or software. Each department or agency has its own needs and requirements, and this is reflected in its choice of platform or platforms. This segmented and fragmented approach extends all the way down to the local city government level.

The growth of free and open-source software has not gone unnoticed by the government. Tough economic times and tax cuts have made many government agencies more cost conscious and freely available software can stretch limited resources even further. Use of Linux, in particular, has grown significantly since the late 1990s. The upshot of this is that experienced game developers should be aware that many agencies would want their graphics-heavy projects to run on OpenGL because of its cross platform nature.

Developer Expectations

Any contract, including the negotiations and the work that follows, can be improved by having proper expectations at the outset. Both sides of the table need to be aware of what they require, what the other party can do to meet those requirements, and what the exchange is worth.

For the retail market, the developer is responsible to the publisher. Similarly, when developing games for a government agency, the developer is responsible to that agency. The agency is Customer 1 (or Customer 0, depending on your preferred base number). The developer is involved because it has experience creating video games, but the ultimate decision maker is the agency. This applies to game design, game content, and anything else.

As mentioned in the previous chapter, Deborah Tillett, President of Break-Away Ltd., a game development company that has created commercial games as well as training games for the government, said that working for a government agency is not that different from working for a retail publisher. In both cases, you have to

- Understand the market you're targeting
- Understand the organization you're working for
- Know who in the organization is ultimately responsible for approving projects.

The due diligence portion of the contract negotiation is familiar to any experienced developer. The publisher sends a representative to meet the development team and confirms that the development team has the experience, team, and resources considered necessary for the upcoming project. Robar pointed out that the government's due diligence can be less interested in the team's experience creating games and more interested in how many Ph.D.s are on the team. Another difference is that while a publisher is looking for a completed project, the government looks for improvement or new knowledge within a particular scope (e.g., "making non-player AI characters appear more humanlike").

Unlike developing retail games, there is often no expectation that the finished game turn a profit. The finished game may be used internally as a training tool, or it may be given away free by the agency as a way to either educate the public or generate attention for the agency, or both. This shift away from the profit motive can reduce or remove the impact of certain features of video games intended as mainstream entertainment. As Bowers and Greb discussed in the "Fire Fighter Training" case study, there is less need for "eye candy," and it may be in the best interest of the project to eliminate any unnecessary features of that sort.

Most work in serious games for the government is commissioned, or work-for-hire. As such, this could be considered an advantage of working for the government because the developer gets to keep all the intellectual property (IP). The developer can then use the IP again in another government project or even a commercial project. Also, if the government agency wants an updated version of the simulation, it has to come back to the developer.

Outside the game development industry, there is little knowledge of what it takes to design a game, staff a development shop, develop a game, and so on. It's possible that the agency may have never overseen the development of any kind of software project before. For these reasons, developers must be able to communicate the entire process clearly and concisely. And then patiently do so again and again, as new decision makers at the agency are brought in, and the ones who've heard it all before forget it at inopportune times. This means, of course, that the developer must understand the process and be able to accurately estimate staffing, time, and budget.

Variable Budgets

Developers who are used to the large (and increasingly larger) budgets of retail games may be prone to "reverse sticker shock" when they discover the budgets available for serious games. At the national government level, the budgets may be comparable to the seven- and eight-digit numbers common in the retail arena. But at the state level, and especially at the county or community level, the budgets will be much smaller. Six-digit budgets are possible, but five-digit budgets will be more common.

With such tight budgets, developers will neither have the luxury of a large project staff nor the option of creating or licensing significant brand-new technology. The developer will have to leverage skilled but minimal staff and available resources. On the other hand, for the future-minded, grow-the-business-oriented developer, these skills will prove valuable, even in retail.

In an interview in *Game Developer*, Doug Whatley, CEO of BreakAway Ltd., pointed out that there could be months between the start of one phase of development and getting paid for it. For that reason, the developer must have enough reserves or existing income to be able to pay expenses for at least a few months, and maybe as long as a year. There is also the added uncertainly factor. "With the government," Whatley said, "you just never know whether something will get funded or not."

More Red Tape

In an interview for the book, *Secrets of the Game Business*, BreakAway's Tillett warned of organizational issues game developers must learn to handle before making the transition from consumer entertainment to serious games: "The back office structure to support government contracting is essential. In other words, the lawyers, separate sales staff, accountants, and so forth are all non-billable overhead that needs to be supported."

Developers working for the government should be aware of the regulations and required paperwork that accompany all government work. The Section 508 accessibility issues mentioned earlier are one example, as are the Federal Acquisition Regulations (FARs). These regulations can impact every aspect of the software development process, so they are not solely the responsibility of the sponsor, content expert, or instructional designer. The developer should be aware of all applicable regulations before starting on the project.

In addition to the FARs, which apply to every project, other industry-specific regulations may apply. Healthcare, and all of its many subcategories, like hospitals and nursing homes, is an example of an industry with a lot of regulations, some of which may apply even to a serious game. DHS has its own supplemental guidelines, the Department of Homeland Security Acquisition Regulation (HSAR). The key stakeholders in the project, though, should be able to point the developer to the necessary FARs and related industry-specific regulations, standards, and practices. That's another reason to keep them involved throughout the development.

Some projects may require the developer to handle classified data, which means that the developer must have a process in place for the handling of that classified data. Security clearances may also be required. If so, the developer will probably have to get a security clearance from that particular branch of the government. While it may be easier to get a security clearance if you already have one, different branches of the government don't accept the clearances granted by other branches. The security clearance processed described in Chapter 4, with its extensive background checks, will be much the same regardless of the particular branch of the government.

When negotiating the contract with the government, the developer should use the same careful procedure used with any other contract. The developer should read the contract carefully and not be afraid to ask questions. The government may want to own the entire IP created for the project, but this is negotiable. It's expected that the government will almost certainly retain ownership of the content of the project, but the developer will want to ensure that it can at least re-use the infrastructure in future projects. The government will have its lawyers inspect the contract and the delivered product. The developer should be prepared to take the same steps.

According to Robar, developers should expect to put a lot more effort into their documentation than they are accustomed to with retail projects. The documentation referred to includes more than just the Help file or player's manual. The initial proposal for the project will need to follow specific guidelines, as will progress reports, and reports that go along with the finished project. Every piece of information related to the project should be tracked and archived: contracts, e-mail, memos, time sheets, everything. Completeness and accuracy are paramount. Also, the developers should know everything about any subcontractors they use. Having this information on hand will prove invaluable if/when the government conducts an audit.

Robar recommended that developers who do not have experience creating and tracking documentation for government projects should consider hiring the necessary talent. There are companies that specialize in exactly this. Though the cost will come out of the project's budget, having such expertise available can ease the transition into doing government work and prevent mistakes. Another approach is to get experience as a subcontractor first. It can be easier for the developer to get into an existing contract as a subcontractor under a company that is already used to dealing with the many standards and regulations, instead of being the prime contractor.

Kent Quirk of CogniToy, whose *MindRover* project for the Defense Acquisition University was discussed in Chapter 4, also stressed the volume of paperwork the company had to fill out and the importance of accurate time and resource accounting. He preferred CogniToy's subcontractor status in dealing with the government because, as the prime contractor, he would have had to deal with even more paperwork.

Furthermore, there are small differences between government agencies in regard to the necessary regulations and procedures. This is another reason to be willing to find and work with people and companies that have experience in government contracting.

Managing Agency Expectations

People who are unfamiliar with game development often have unrealistic expectations. Developers need to help government agencies and stakeholders understand the following:

- They don't know how games are designed and made, which is why they're hiring a game developer.
- Creating a game that looks just like the latest blockbuster hit for the latest console hardware is well outside the budget range available for this project.

- Game design is a creative process, and therefore hard to schedule in an absolute manner. That is, expect it to take more or less (but probably more) time than estimated.

The first point can be a touchy issue. No one likes to be told they don't know something, and nothing makes managers more nervous than overseeing a project where they aren't familiar with the required processes. So developers should take the time to talk to the agency managers and teach them the basics of the game development process. The managers don't need to be able to open their own development shop, but they should at least be conversant with the software project lifecycle, including concepts like milestones, playtesting, and so on.

The second point is covered by a proper education about the first point. Once managers realize that AAA retail titles require millions of dollars, dozens or hundreds of people, and years of effort to produce, they quickly adjust their goals for the project and become more willing to use off-the-shelf, third-party components over fully custom solutions. Or maybe they go back and find/acquire additional funding.

The last point can also be a sensitive issue, but, like the second, can be managed by proper expectations on both sides. The agency must be flexible enough to allow for some variance in the schedule. On the other hand, the developer must be willing to put forth the effort to properly gauge the project from the beginning and be disciplined enough to keep the project moving.

As game development proceeds, it might be necessary for the developer and the agency to decide on changes from the original vision. A single-purpose simulation with a narrow scope won't suffer the same evolution of design as a video game, but there will be changing requirements and adjustments as the product comes to fruition. New uses and approaches will be discovered the more the product is used. Running into the limitations of available technology (such as the 3D engine or the networking code) and feedback from playtesting are also common reasons for this kind of project re-assessment. The important thing is that the issues be recognized and dealt with quickly. Delaying decisions of this sort are never good for the project.

CONCLUSION

At first glance, developing serious games for the government may seem to be very different than developing for traditional video game publishers, and it is. In particular, the regulations that cover government contracts can be a huge burden. However, there are as many similarities as differences, and with a bit of effort to learn the particulars there is no reason why a developer who is successful in the private sector couldn't leverage that success in the public sector.

One of the things that must be learned is that there is more than one public sector. Government agencies range from the national level to the state or province level, all the way down to the local city council. Developers that focus only at the national level may miss out on a good opportunity at the state level, or even in their own community.

Greater participation in the civic processes at all levels could prove to be a huge boon to the game development industry as a whole. Game developers will see themselves as more directly affected by government and be more involved. At the same time, politicians may learn that game developers are interested in more than just shooting space aliens and promoting violence. More understanding on both sides of the debate can only improve the perception on each side.

In the next chapter, we'll look at serious games in education.

CHAPTER

EDUCATIONAL GAMES

Education based on the methods of question, answer, and discussion dates back to ancient Greece and the dawn of civilization. Over the millennia since then, education has adopted books, movies, and even television as these new media proved their effectiveness. These tools improved both the reach and effectiveness of education. Games in general, and video games in particular, are now in the process of proving their effectiveness as tools of training and teaching. Gradually, the acceptance of games as another educational tool is growing.

The acceptance of games in the classroom is still hardly universal, though. Skeptics look askance at games, especially video games, demanding proof that the games teach anything useful, and asking how well the games teach compared to more traditional methods. However, every new teaching tool has undergone this scrutiny, even computers and, more recently, the Internet. Today no one questions the value of computers in the classroom, and the Internet is still creating new educational opportunities. Video games will also prove their value.

In this chapter, we will review the history of games in the classroom, both video games and other types of games, and how the combination of games and computers are being used now and how they might be used in the future. The attitudes of educators and parents will also be reviewed. We will also cover the peculiar issues of developing serious games for use in schools, including integration of games into lesson plans and testing programs.

GAMES IN THE CLASSROOM

In his 1969 book, *Serious Games*, Clark Abt described the 1960s Avalon Hill game, *Grand Strategy*, as it was shown to junior high school students. The game, which simulates some of the events of World War I, was played by the students through their morning classes. The game unfolded much like WWI, with an entanglement of alliances between students that led to global war. Just before lunch, the students were told they would get a chance to play the game again in the afternoon. Some students went to the school library during lunch to study the history of the Great War. The afternoon game, played with the experience of the morning and the results of the "active learning" (the self-motivated research of WWI in the school library), resulted in a peaceful compromise.

Abt theorized in that 1969 edition of his book that a growing shortage of teachers would lead to more educational use of games in the classroom. Looking back from 1984, when updating the book, he observed that while there remained a shortage of teachers, the market for education games was, at that time, still minimal when compared to the market for entertainment products. In those 15 years, there had been little change. In the two decades since then, however, fueled by the powerful combination of the personal computer and the Internet, there have been some changes.

Personal Computers, the Internet, and Edutainment

The development of personal computers rode on the coattails of the new game consoles, like the Atari 2600 devices, that hooked up to TVs in the home. The simple input peripherals, usually either a joystick or paddle, limited the educational possibilities of early game consoles. Still, games like *Basic Programming* and *Fun with Numbers* were created for the Atari 2600. The lesser-known Fairchild/ Zircon Channel F console also had educational cartridges teaching math and programming.

Personal computers, especially the Apple II series, the Commodore 64, and later the Apple Macintosh, made the move from the home to the classroom in the middle 1980s. Apple Computer, in particular, worked hard to get computers into classrooms, launching the Classrooms of Tomorrow program in 1985. The Learning Company (acquired by Riverdeep in 2001) was started in 1979 by Ann McCormick with the idea of combining reading and writing with a cartoon character, which resulted in the popular Reader Rabbit and Rocky's Boots series of products. Through all of these various efforts, personal computers became a fixture of the modern classroom.

In the 1990s, PCs became "multi-media," supporting high-color displays, quality sound and music playback, and large secondary storage, like hard drives and CD-ROM drives. PCs that had once been the domain of business and productivity software, like spreadsheets and word processors, could now play games, music, and more. Combined with falling hardware prices, PCs moved into homes and schools around the world.

Educational software boomed as parents justified the cost of their new PCs by purchasing just about anything labeled "educational." Sales of typing games, math games, reading games, and chess games surged. Even Mario, the plumber from Nintendo, had a typing game, *Mario Teaches Typing*. In his book, *Digital Game-Based Learning*, Marc Prensky talked about John Kernan, Chairman and CEO of Lightspan (now a part of PLATO Learning). In the mid-1990s, Kernan was able to raise $50 million from Sony, Microsoft, and other sources to develop game-based learning CDs to run on the Sony Playstation video game consoles.

Kernan started Lightspan primarily to sell to schools, but with little time to use such technology in schools, the home, and more specifically, the parents, became the primary target. This changed both the marketing approach and the design of the software. By targeting the home, Lightspan's educational CDs needed to be entertaining in order to compete with television and other video games. Unlike when they're at school, children can choose to do whatever they want at home. With an emphasis on fun, and trying to mimic the look of video games and using characters that kids would relate to, Lightspan's goal was not to teach new material but to act as a reinforcement or a way of reviewing the material. A 2000 report by Lightspan's research division showed that students using Lightspan's products saw a 30 percent increase in standardized test scores.

The boom in educational games and CDs waned as the Internet became the new focus, and the category of educational games and software evolved into what is known as "edutainment." Even more than the new focus on the Internet, edutainment's credibility was eroded by a rash of poorly conceived, poorly designed games. Still, in 2000 edutainment had become a $1.6 billion annual market.

Since 2000, there has been even more growth in educational toys, games, and software. Companies such as Leapfrog have created a vast array of products that merge computer technology with educational goals like reading and mathematics.

So far, though, there has been more acceptance of edutainment by parents, who use the games and toys to prepare their children for school, than by teachers. This is reflected in the marketing campaigns used, which show kids having fun while their parents look on proudly. Teachers, as education professionals, tend to be more skeptical of the claims of edutainment. In many cases, they still need to be convinced about the efficacy of games in the classroom.

Japan in particular has had a history of commercial simulation products, which are arguably educational, even if they were built as entertainment products. Such simulation games range over a wide variety of topics. For example, there have been games like *Densha de Go!*, a train operating game, and *Power Shovel in Norou!*, a power shovel operating game, that have been huge hits in Japan. There have also been many titles concerning music (see Figure 6.1). *Bravo Music* lets players pretend to be a conductor while *Drum Master* teaches drum techniques to players. Finally, tycoon games like *Conveni*, a convenience store tycoon game, and *Yoshino-ya*, about running a beef rice bowl restaurant, have taught players about business.

FIGURE 6.1

Drum Master

© Sande Chen. Used with Permission.

Why Use Games in the Classroom?

Combined with the Internet, serious games offer a significant opportunity for educators. According to the National Center for Education Statistics March 2005 report, "Computer Technology in the Public School Classroom: Teacher Perspectives," which summarizes the results of several studies, the percentage of public schools in the United States with access to the Internet increased to 99 percent in 2002, up from 35 percent in 1994. Where there is Internet access, there is a computer of some sort. And where there are computers, games can't be far behind, or too far out of reach.

Games—the New Teachers

Games are being shown as effective teaching tools, and developers are working with teachers to integrate those games into the classroom. Video games have penetrated the mass culture to almost the same level that television has and have even had a measurable effect on the number of television viewers. Moreover, the learning styles developed from video games are vastly different from those expected in traditional classrooms.

When John Beck and Mitchell Wade surveyed 2500 young professionals for their book, *Got Game: How the Gamer Generation Is Reshaping Business Forever*, they found that those who described themselves as regular gamers were more creative, more ambitious, and more optimistic about their abilities and circumstances. The authors cited a Discovery Channel documentary that compared video games to a "simplified world" that emphasizes tangible results while providing constant, critical feedback, calling that a well-designed training environment.

William Winn, head of the Learning Center at the University of Washington's Human Interface Technology Laboratory, as quoted in Beck and Wade's book, said that kids who grew up gaming think differently from their parents (who didn't play video games) and will grow into adults who can process information in new ways. Further, Beck and Wade observed that "gaming has created an entirely different learning style." Specifically, this learning style

- "Aggressively ignores" the structure and format of formal instruction.

- Is built on extensive trial and error, with a "failure is nearly free; you just push play again" mentality.

- Includes input and instruction from peers (other gamers), not authority figures.

- Emphasizes "just in time" learning, with new skills and information picked up just before they are needed.

James Paul Gee explained the advantages of video games as learning devices in his book, *What Video Games Have to Teach Us about Learning and Literacy*. "If the principles of learning in good video games *are* good," he wrote in the introduction, "then better theories of learning are embedded in the video games many children in elementary and particularly in high school play than in the schools they attend." He went on to say that such a theory of learning might be a better fit for the modern world than the traditional methods.

Beck and Wade also reported that as early as the mid-1980s, UCLA researchers had established that "students who also played video games showed improved cognitive skills, including improved visualization and mental maps. Other research has found improved visual memory in children as young as four years old as a result of playing video games."

With the adoption of video games in the classroom, teachers can adjust to this new learning style and better prepare children for the modern world. In his book, *Re-imagine!*, Tom Peters quoted psychologist Edward de Bono: "Children should be taught in an active way by doing things and playing games. It's very different than what is taught in schools, which involves sitting back and absorbing information."

Indeed, a study from the NTL Institute for Applied Behavioral Sciences in Alexandria, Virginia found that the learning retention rates go up to 75 to 80 percent when catering to the learning style of gamers, compared to the 5 percent learning retention rate of lecture-based instruction.

No Child Left without a Gamepad

Decades before video games with varying levels of difficulty became mass culture, Abt saw the opportunity for games to provide instruction that is "custom-fit" to individual student capabilities. Even students in the same nominal grade are at different levels. Some are above average and some are below average. This is especially true in public schools, which have a broader spectrum of students. Games can be tailored to match these finer gradations of ability.

In addition, Abt contended that games could motivate poor learners who have skills that are not brought to light using conventional teaching methods. Games might even identify those skills in students that otherwise might be written off as not bright or sub par. In the same manner, shy and withdrawn children could become active and communicative within the context of a game.

There are, after all, different types of learning. In the 1960s, psychologist Benjamin Bloom created "Bloom's Taxonomy" of three different types of learning: cognitive, affective, and psychomotor. More recently, Mark Tennant divided learning into attitude, skills, and knowledge (or ASK). Adding to the debate, Howard Gardner posited seven different types of intelligence or knowledge: logical-mathematical, linguistic, spatial, musical, kinesthetic, interpersonal, and intrapersonal. These are just three examples of the ways that learning has been categorized.

However you subdivide education, though, serious games have the potential to explore different types of learning, much more than lectures, training videos, or even books can. Abt spoke of a study that showed, using written tests before and after a game, that students demonstrated greater learning from the game than what is usually attained by a lecture in the same amount of time. "A game," he stated, "greatly accelerates the sequence of activities being simulated. Game-playing provides an immediate reward to the individual who makes a correct decision, while the student who fails to do so knows his mistake at once and can correct his error."

This description aligns serious games with a philosophy called *constructivism*. Constructivism has been adopted in many fields over the past decades, including education. Kathleen Iverson, in her book *E-learning Games: Interactive Learning Strategies for Digital Delivery*, summed up a few of the more common definitions: "Constructivism is an educational philosophy founded on the premise that by reflecting on our experiences, we construct our own understanding of the world in which we live." Prensky put it this way: "Constructivists believe that a person learns best when he or she actively 'constructs' ideas and relationships in their own minds based on experiments that they do, rather than being told." Serious games provide a way for students to not just memorize facts, but also to gain experience and create their own internalized "model" for how what they learn is applied to their life.

Clark Aldrich, in his book *Simulations and the Future of Learning*, said that much of what is taught today falls into a linear pattern. First one thing is taught, and then the next, and the next, and so on. Often this progression is based on what is seen as the most logical way for the material to be presented. It's not uncommon, though, that the order be arbitrarily assigned. A better approach, according to Aldrich, is to present the material in a "cyclical, linear, and open-ended" manner. This lets the student establish the order of presentation and repeat those parts he or she doesn't get the first time, or just enjoys. Just as someone learning tennis practices over and over, the cyclical approach lets the student practice and map out what's necessary. Also, an open-ended process encourages exploration and creativity.

Abt also saw games as a mechanism for demonstrating just learned knowledge and skills within their proper context. "Once a student is in a game, he is unlikely to withdraw from the other participants or to ignore the moves they make," Abt wrote. "His understanding of the principles involved is therefore reinforced not only in what he does but also in what his opponent and/or partner does." Games further reinforce the mastery of skills and concepts by dramatizing the relationship or interaction of issues studied.

The Future of Games in the Classroom

To those of us with an interest in serious games, it seems inevitable that in the future games will have a bigger role in the classroom. As indicated by survey result 6.1, 95 percent of respondents predicted that serious games would become a standard part of school curriculum.

Serious Games Survey Result 6.1

Question: Do you think serious games will become a standard part of education/training curriculum?

95.24%	Yes
4.76%	No

(Survey Note: 63 Respondents)

When asked why or why not, the respondents gave a variety of reasons. Many of the responses were variations of "This generation is used to getting its information digitally" and "is too media literate and expectant to tolerate the lower levels of interactivity and engagement that traditional education provides."

A number insisted on the caveat that while serious games may become a standard part of education and training, it won't happen soon. "The public's acceptance [and interest in serious games] is too low at the moment," said one. "It's going to take a long while (until the Gamer Generation is running the show)," said another, "but eventually it will get there."

Overall, as might be expected, the responses talked about the benefits of serious games, including

- Ability to model complex systems
- Higher engagement with the material
- Advantages of interactivity when learning
- Similarities to constructivist teaching methods
- Cost savings by reducing skill training time and less expensive than doing the same training in a real world setting

Already, students of all ages have found certain commercial off-the-shelf games to be beneficial in the classroom. Monte Cristo Games created their management simulation titles, including *Wall Street Trader*, *Start-up*, and *Airport Tycoon* as entertainment, leveraging publisher-funded development to create a series of simulation games based around a core engine. Despite being designed as entertainment, university students, especially those in business school, have found Monte Cristo's products to be useful for training.

Games like *Zoo Tycoon* and *Dance Dance Revolution* are being used in some schools. *Dance Dance Revolution*, for example, has been used in physical education classes in schools in the United States, United Kingdom, and Europe. As the potential for serious games becomes known, it's likely that more retail games will include features and support material so that they can be used more easily in the classroom.

2005's *Pax Warrior* is an example of a game designed specifically for the classroom and could be indicative of future trends. *Pax Warrior* tackles a tough topic: the genocide in Rwanda from the viewpoint of UN peacekeepers. The game provides a dark lesson in modern history while also demonstrating the choices faced by the UN peacekeepers during that period. The designer, Andreas Ua'Siaghail, wanted to show that for every choice there are troubling consequences. The educational simulation promotes this idea in dramatic fashion.

Although video games have made some headway into the classroom, the eventual inevitability of video games in the classroom will depend on teachers and school administrators. If teachers can be convinced of their usefulness and can easily bring the games to bear on the day-to-day issues of modern education, they will begin pressuring the school systems from the inside to adopt games. Key to the acceptance of teachers, though, is proof, backed up by solid research, that the games actually do a better job than current methods.

Research into Games and Education

There is still very little solid, irrefutable evidence of the effectiveness of games in the classroom and how serious games compare to more traditional methods. Eric Klopfer, Associate Professor at the Massachusetts Institute of Technology (MIT), remarked that the question, "Are games educational?" is too broad. Clearly, some games are educational and some are not so educational. Research is still in the early stages, but some of the research shows real promise and demonstrates the potential benefits of games.

At least anecdotally, students have shown to be more motivated when given games to learn with. However, more than motivation is required for learning, and anecdotal evidence is hard to quantify. Furthermore, the other educational benefits of serious games are less understood. This is changing, though, with new studies being conducted every year.

Three significant areas in which research is being conducted are assessment of learning, cost per student, and the potential uses of serious games. Assessment of learning examines how well the student learned what was being taught. The cost per student, or return on investment of serious games, is important because unless or until the cost per student proves to be less overall than existing methods, the adoption rate of games in education will remain low. Similarly, there is interest in how extensively serious games can be used across a variety of disciplines.

In his 2004 presentation to the Serious Games Summit in Washington, D.C., "What Happens when Games Go into Any Classroom Situation?", Kurt Squire, Assistant Professor at the University of Wisconsin at Madison, pointed out that as an industry, game developers, academics, and educational professionals still don't know how to make a good serious game nor do they fully understand how players interpret the content of a game. Despite their apparent usefulness, games, he said, are not grounded in any theory of learning.

At the same conference, in his presentation, "Assessment and the Future of Fluid Learning Environments," Aaron Thibault, Research and Development Coordinator at the Digital Media Collaboratory in the IC^2 Institute at the University of Texas at Austin, talked about what he called "fluid learning environments," that is, serious games or other learning systems that adapted to the students over time. He saw these fluid learning environments as coming at the intersection of system intelligence, human learning, and system architecture. Again, the future proved hard to predict.

Thibault also talked about the need to construct a framework for assessment of game learning, based on cognitive psychology, game design, machine learning, neurobiology, and educational theory. Until some methodology can be created and agreed upon, it will be necessary to "keep humans in the loop." That is, someone will have to be present to administer the necessary tests. Full automation of testing, he added, is not expected to occur for some years.

Getting into the Classroom Case Study—*Power Politics III*

Power Politics III is a U.S. presidential election campaign simulator developed by Kellogg Creek Software, an independent game development company in Happy Valley, Oregon. The player chooses the candidates who will run, selecting from real presidential candidates dating all the way back to 1960.

The player then manages the campaign of his or her chosen candidate, from start to finish, by hiring staffers, overseeing advertising, and trying to control the topic of the campaign. Though designed to be an entertaining experience, *Power Politics III* provides a detailed view of U.S. democracy and the electoral process and has been used by teachers and college professors to explore the electoral process.

Power Politics III is based on the original *Power Politics* game, also designed by Randy Chase, President of Kellogg Creek Software, and *The Doonesbury Election Game* created for the 1996 U.S. presidential campaign. Leveraging the research and development of the previous versions, Chase said, development of *Power Politics III* took a small team less than a year to build.

In spring 2005, Kellogg Creek Software changed its licensing, making *Power Politics III* free to educators who wanted to use the game in their classrooms. The company had always offered a discounted price for teachers and professors, but it had sold only a few that way. "Schools are struggling for funding," Chase said. If an independent developer wants to sell to schools, it's difficult to sell directly to teachers or school systems. Thus Kellogg Creek Software's new model for the educational version of the game is to give it away free to teachers who want to use it and seek corporate sponsorship to provide increased revenue, greater exposure, and so on.

The company's goal with *Power Politics III* is to "find creative ways to build new alliances." Having found little support from the retail game publishers, Kellogg Creek Software is branching out, forging partnerships with non-traditional entities outside the game industry, who have not had much presence in the video games arena before. There is "lots of interest in the non-game world," Chase said. Many corporations, for example, are looking to tap into the power of video games. Independent developers, he added, "have the freedom and flexibility to try" these new alliances and partnerships, unlike big retail publishers, who have a vested interest in the status quo.

Corporate sponsorship comes in a variety of forms. At its simplest, the corporate sponsor allows the game developer to use the corporation's name in marketing materials. The announcement of the new corporate sponsor can be an event worthy of a press release and generate exposure for the game.

Corporate sponsorships can also provide valuable leverage for getting the attention of other corporations who might be interested in supporting such an effort. "Building credibility is the hardest part," Chase said. He credited the support of *The Christian Science Monitor*, a national newspaper, for getting *Power Politics III* endorsed by the Rock The Vote campaign.

Chase said that the types of companies he has approached for sponsorship are search engines, technology companies, hardware manufacturers, and consumer products companies. "All of those companies are looking to get their names in front of high school students," Chase pointed out. In some cases, if it seems relevant, the sponsorship includes content from the company. An example Chase gave was that in *Power Politics III*, the headlines that scroll in the game could come from *The Christian Science Monitor*.

A more controversial form of corporate sponsorship includes product placement and other product marketing messages within the game. "We have to be careful," Chase said, because there is a fine line between profit from additional revenue and offending the educational world. Teachers understand that these types of games and other educational materials have to be funded, but they are very resistant to blatant advertising.

To help teachers use the game in the classroom, Kellogg Creek Software collects stories of how other teachers have used the game and provides those as examples on its Web site. Examples include having the student run a campaign, and then write a report on how it progressed. Other writing assignments could be about planning a campaign and choosing strategies beforehand. "Not all education has to be formal, structured learning," Chase said. With that in mind, Kellogg Creek Software tries to make the game as flexible as possible so that it can be used in a variety of ways. There's also a private discussion forum on the Web site for teachers to share ideas with each other directly.

A deluxe version of *Power Politics III* is available for sale. It features fantasy elections that would allow players to pit historically inaccurate candidates against each other, like Hillary Clinton versus George Bush (see Figure 6.2). The next election is coming, and Chase feels there is a competitive advantage to having the product seen in high schools and universities across the United States.

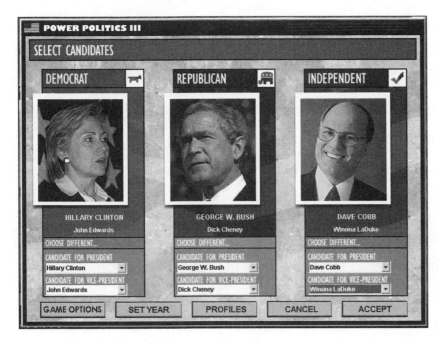

FIGURE 6.2

Power Politics III

© Kellogg Creek Software. Used with Permission.

DEVELOPING EDUCATIONAL GAMES

Some years ago, Henry Jenkins and Kurt Squire, co-directors of the Education Arcade, surveyed students at MIT for their opinions about educational games. Many of the responses were as expected, that most educational games were not very good games and that those games could not match commercial games in terms of the graphics, audio, and gameplay. Despite this dismal showing, though, Jenkins and Squire concluded that "it's not that good educational games can't exist; it's that people making them usually don't understand the medium."

Chase agreed. He said, "There's an element in education that thinks they can develop their own games." Unfortunately, not all educators are good game designers. Experienced game developers are needed to bring serious games into the classroom. This isn't a one-sided equation, though, because game developers will need to collaborate closely with education professionals to ensure accuracy and pedagogical value.

Design Issues

The future of any sort of game in the classroom will be determined by teachers at all levels of education. If teachers do not see the benefits of serious games or consider them a hindrance, the future could be bleak. The parents of students are another important group to consider.

Aldrich offered the following criterion for educational simulations:

1. In-game scenarios and situations must be both authentic and relevant.

2. These scenarios should tap into the emotions and compel the students to act.

3. The scenarios should provide a sense of unrestricted options.

4. The scenarios should be replayable.

Many of the design issues that affect serious games for education were covered in Chapter 3, "Serious Games Design and Development Issues." Here we will focus on the concerns of teachers and parents and how those concerns might affect the design of serious games for education.

The Concerns of Teachers

Teachers have a history of distrusting mass culture media, going back to the 19th century and "penny dreadfuls," as the popular paperback novels of the time were called. Movies, televisions, comic books, and rock-n-roll music have all drawn the ire of educators who feared the end of literacy and an appreciation for the classics. Video games are only the most recent threat to Western Civilization.

This doesn't apply to all teachers, of course. Teachers aren't even unified in their beliefs about what constitutes education and learning. Constructivism, mentioned earlier in this chapter, is an example of only one theory of learning, and even that philosophy is subdivided. There is mild constructivism, radical constructivism, and more, each one emphasizing different roles and priorities for teachers, students, and even society. Plus, constructivism is not the only significant philosophy of pedagogy.

At an educational conference in 1965, Abt reported that the former head of the American Federation of Teachers said games would keep teachers too busy to do their jobs and were also a threat to their jobs. Forty years later, these fears are still evident. He described the responses of teachers to games as enthusiastic, ambivalent, or violently opposed. Some thought that if games were used extensively, the teacher would become a coach and a research director rather than a lecturer and disciplinarian. "In a class where games are used," Abt wrote, "the teacher must learn to give brief but very intensive analyses and explanations, interspersed with longer periods of observations of student experiments and occasional coaching remarks. This is entirely different from the continuous pattern of doctrinaire topical material transferred from textbooks to the teacher's mind to the teacher's mouth to the students' pencils."

Further, Abt talked about teachers objecting to games teaching immoral behavior. For example, in *Empire*, a game simulating 18th-century trade between England, Europe, and the various American colonies, players could engage in activities such as bribing officials, slave-trading, and smuggling. Students delighted in the illegal activities, to the dismay of the teachers. If games teach, the question goes, then how can we avoid teaching immoral or incorrect things in games? What if the games teach the wrong lessons? Abt pointed out that this concern is not limited to games because the same issue exists with books and lectures.

More recently, Klopfer said he had seen two basic camps. The first group is the teachers who are excited when they see the potential of serious games. On the other side are those who say, "We don't want to fall prey to the 'education has to be fun' mentality." The challenge for game developers is moving serious games from the good idea stage and into something useful.

Also, teachers already have full schedules and a long list of responsibilities. Any new tool or method either must replace or integrate with an existing tool or method. Or, as Klopfer elaborated, some teachers tend to feel, "If you insert something new into the classroom, something else has to leave."

In his presentation to the 2005 Serious Games Summit at the Game Developers Conference, John Kirriemuir gave the following list of teacher concerns with using games in the classroom, compiled from a survey of teachers in the United Kingdom:

- Potential negative reaction from other teachers and parents.

- Lack of examples of how games have been and could be used.

- Fear that students are possibly learning less than with traditional methods.

- Lack of validation of commercial games as learning tools.

- Worry that school computers are insufficient to run modern games.

These concerns are born from a variety of sources. Kirriemuir listed the ups and downs of the edutainment market over the years: articles in the press where video games are portrayed as the decline of education, educators who resist change, and educational funding organizations that are uncertain about the future of video games in the classroom. All of these have generated concern in teachers. He also pointed out that retail video game publishers often present themselves as edgy, radical, and anti-establishment when they target the hardcore players. Such publishers see themselves and their games as the polar opposite of schools and education, which they consider boring.

In addition, Kirriemuir reported that there have also been some incorrect assumptions about the role of the teacher when using games. He re-emphasized the fear that teachers will be marginalized or replaced by games. There is also some concern about whether the students are learning the material presented or just learning how to play the game.

Like professionals in all fields, teachers face their jobs every day using the tools they have been trained to use, and these methods have proven successful for them in the past. They are interested in new tools and new methods, but only if they can see how using those tools can help them do their job better, faster, and more effectively. Fortunately, there has been some effort in regard to these issues.

John Kirriemuir listed these four requirements of games from teachers:

- **Examples from other teachers.** Because it's not always obvious how a game can or should be used in the classrooms, the developer should provide examples, or work with teachers to create examples, of how the serious game is intended to be used.

- **"Lite" games.** Games for the classroom should not have long, full-motion video (FMV) sequences or cut scenes that interrupt the game. Also, the games should have all advertising and features that aren't relevant to the classroom removed. Finally, the game should be playable from any point the teacher chooses.

- **Maintain accuracy.** The simulation and information presented by the game must be as accurate as possible and should avoid controversy where possible. On the other hand, the game should remove the boring parts that take up so much of real life.

- **Support homework.** As has been mentioned before, teachers need to have the game start at a point that is directly relevant to the day's lesson. Teachers want to start off where they were before or where the students can solve a particular problem. Also, teachers need to be able to assign homework and tasks.

Kirriemuir's presentation focused on commercial, off-the-shelf (COTS) games. These are games like *Power Politics III* that were created for retail sale but might also be used for educational purposes. However, his points are equally applicable to games created specifically for the classroom.

Developers need to think about how to integrate the serious games they design into the classroom, Klopfer said. What do you expect the student/player to learn from the game? How do you expect them to learn it? And how do you integrate play time with time for critical thinking? Having a clear distinction between learning and play has been a popular approach, and, according to Klopfer, is often the worst possible design. Playing and learning need to be integrated. Students need to be able to reflect on the experience of the game.

The Concerns of Parents

Parents have always been concerned about the education of their children, and they have looked for ways to augment the education their children receive from school. As we discussed earlier, this concern has been one of the driving forces of the growth of edutainment software.

Seeking to give their children an edge in the increasingly competitive 21st-century world, parents are taking very active roles in their children's education. Many parents want their children to have a head start and are starting their children's education long before those children would be starting school. They also want to introduce advanced material to their children who are already in the education system. Other parents want to add to or shore up the education their children receive, either because they are unhappy with the school or because their child has a learning disability.

Whether they are looking to improve their children's academic performance at school or have taken over their children's education completely, via homeschooling, parents have many of the same concerns as teachers. Like teachers, parents want some kind of proof that the child is actually learning what the game purports to teach.

Finally, there is one last group, besides parents, teachers, and administrators, who may have to be convinced about the effectiveness of video games in the classroom: students. Just like everyone else involved, students have expectations of what they should be doing in school. Modern students, Klopfer said, are used to passive education, and they may resist changing that and resent having their entertainment of choice converted into an educational experience.

Games at All Levels of Education

Serious games can be used for education at all levels, from preschool and elementary school, through middle school and high school, into colleges and universities, and even into the job market. One game doesn't have to support all of those levels, but some might be able to.

Abt suggested one way an educator might teach students about the U.S. Constitution. Rather than just reading the Constitution and the story of how the Constitution was written, students could instead participate in a Constitutional Convention-style game. They can then see the process by which certain articles were included in the document and others weren't. The more traditional reading can be left for homework, reserving the classroom time for the game. With proper selection of the issues and articles debated, such a game could be used in American history classes at nearly any level of education, from grade school through secondary schools and universities.

In late 2004, Linden Lab, creator of the 3D digital world *Second Life*, announced *Campus: Second Life*, a program that allowed college level classes to use the tools and environment of *Second Life* as a virtual classroom. Building on the realistic physical simulation, 3D modeling, and economic and social systems of the game, *Campus: Second Life* was meant to provide students with a collaborative framework to experiment in real time with everything from urban planning to game design to the formation of social communities. Already, some university professors have gravitated to the service, encouraging students to create businesses and test entrepreneurial skills.

At the university level, Klopfer said, professors have proven to be more open to serious games than the administration. He has used *SimCity* and *Civilization* in his own classes, and plans to do more.

Keeping It Age-Appropriate

Though the hardcore player market tends to get the bulk of the attention from game developers, there have always been games intended for all ages, even young children who still have a hard time pushing the mouse around. Prensky called such games "baby programming" because they are intended for children aged three or under. There's even "lapware," which gets its name from the parent having to hold the child in his or her lap to play the game.

As an educational tool, *Power Politics III* targets high school and university students, Chase said. However, the game has also been picked up by middle school teachers for use in their classrooms. "There's nothing age-*in*-appropriate in the game," Chase said. When designing the game, he tried to treat all of the candidates in the game, both living and late, with "a world of respect." This meant leaving out the tabloid headlines and stories that plagued some of the candidates. "I don't know which one of those candidates is your hero," Chase added, "so I treat them all with a lot of respect."

Even though *Power Politics III* is based on real political issues and includes an arsenal of typical political "dirty tricks" for the player to use, the game is kept lighthearted, and the less savory elements of politics are presented "tongue-in-cheek." The reason the dirty tricks were included was to show their impact on the campaign, not to degrade the candidate or to promote the designer's own political views. As a result, a wider range of students can play the game.

Another advantage of this approach, Chase said, is that it keeps the game from dating itself. Specific events referenced in a game cause the game to become dated.

Combining Fun and Learning

Klopfer referred to the content part of serious games as the "Trojan horse." In other words, as the student plays the game he or she learns the desired subject, whether the student intended to or not. If video games encourage ways to make education more engaging, that's good. After all, it wouldn't be bad if all learning were engaging, such that students wanted to learn the topic. Fun isn't the only way to do this, of course, but it's a built-in advantage of video games. Besides fun, the games should promote higher-order thinking skills, such as teamwork, data collection, and analysis.

Today's students, said Chase, have a "whole different view on technology." They don't just accept technology; they demand it. Fun is a critical factor for them. A boring game, educational or not, will be avoided. However, he added, "fun is the tool." Fun serious games will never replace teachers, but such games can stimulate much interest and excitement.

Another approach to fun in educational games is discussed in the "Hidden Agenda Contest" case study later in this chapter.

Measurable Results and Reporting

As we discussed in Chapter 3, serious games have additional considerations that distinguish them from entertainment games: testing. Teachers, the school administration, and, more recently, the national government, need to know whether or not the student has actually learned the content of the serious game.

How do we measure what has been learned? That question was asked over and over at the Serious Games Summit in Washington, D.C., in 2004. "There is no magic bullet," Thibault declared at the beginning of his presentation, mentioned earlier. The nature of serious games as "fluid learning environments," or learning environments that adapt to learners over time, makes it difficult to assess what the player learned, how quickly it was learned, and so on.

Currently, assessment is limited to more traditional testing approaches and self-assessments given by the players before and after playing. Classroom testing usually happens after the presentation of the class material. With the efficacy of serious games still being determined, though, it's important for testing to occur both before and after the game. Without a gauge of the student's knowledge or abilities both before and after, it's impossible to know if anything was learned—and just because the player thinks he learned something doesn't mean that he actually did.

Prensky called the current testing approach the "tell-test" system of education. In tell-test education, somebody who knows more than the students is telling them what they have to learn, and then testing them on it. This approach continues to be popular for a number of reasons. Perhaps the most important reasons are, first, that it's a rather simple approach and relatively fast. Standardized, computer- readable tests help reduce a teacher's workload. Secondly, education is a bureaucracy, and bureaucracies are notoriously slow to change.

Regardless of whether or not the developer agrees with the current emphasis on testing, it's a part of modern education and will have to be included in serious games. Fortunately, not all of the methods of assessment need to be integrated into the game itself. The game should make it easy to use any of them, though.

The most obvious way to assess content knowledge is using traditional types of testing, such as multiple-choice questions, either in the game or out of it. Other options are interviews, based around particular problems, general problem solving, surveys, or a mixture of observation, tests, and interviews. On the other hand, traditional methods of grading and testing may be problematic. Does a student's grade really reflect the student's progress in the material or the teacher's abilities? These questions underscore the difficulty faced by designers of serious games.

Clark Quinn, author of the book *Engaging Learning: Designing e-Learning Simulation Games*, said in an interview that proper design of the training simulation can make assessment of learning quite simple. In short, if the student achieves the goal condition within the serious game, they have passed the test. The challenge then becomes to create the scenario for the simulation such that it cannot be successfully overcome with simple, random trial and error.

Aldrich also brought up the question of the proper grading system for an open-ended simulation. In the game *Roller Coaster Tycoon*, for example, one metric is customer satisfaction. However, Aldrich then pointed out that players could improve their customer satisfaction by drowning the unhappy guests. In cases like this, do you, as a teacher, punish the student for exploiting a loophole in the system? Or reward them for the creative use of available resources and metrics? And does either option present a desirable, preferred outcome or lesson?

Games designed for retail don't have to prove their players are learning anything, and so they don't face the same challenge when creating their scenarios, missions, or levels. The burden is on the serious game designer to make sure that these kinds of loopholes don't exist, while still maintaining the possibility for other, more beneficial emergent behaviors.

Tests and testing are the problems tackled by psychometrics, the study of measuring the brain. With roots in psychology and cognitive science, psychometric researchers are trying to develop assessment techniques for measuring mental capabilities, such as thinking and knowledge. "It's the job of the psychometrician," said Jonathan Ferguson, Interaction Designer for EduMetrics, a research company in Provo, Utah, to verify that a test "is measuring what it's designed to measure."

Ferguson expressed disappointment with many of the educational products and edutainment games available today. Not only are they not using accurate metrics in tracking the supposed learning, but many of these companies are assuming that their software is helping, when it's possible that the software can be damaging to the intellectual growth of the child or student.

Figuring out if a student learned the subject matter is a difficult task, Ferguson went on, and different people have their peculiar sensitivities. It's possible to discourage someone from an area by engaging with them in a way that is harmful to their willingness to participate in that area. How the material is presented to the student and how retention or understanding of that material is assessed can have a profound effect on how the student reacts to similar material in the future.

Computers and video games are uniquely positioned to change how testing is done, Ferguson said. With a video game, the teacher won't be saying, "Play this game. There will be a test at the end." It's possible that there will be no need for a separate quiz or test. The teacher, or the software itself, could identify by the behavior of a student in the game whether he or she understood something or not. After all, software has the ability to assess the player while that player is interacting with the software, and this assessment can be provided to the teacher. "That's the direction assessment should be taking," Ferguson added.

Squire stressed the need for more research on how people play and learn and how they learn while playing. "We tend to use technology to reproduce what we're already doing," he said. An example of this is in the early uses of film and video to simply play back prerecorded lectures. Games and traditional schools function very differently, and developers and educators may need to revisit their theories of learning and testing before they can make any progress in this area.

Working with Educators

Educators represent a huge resource for designers of serious games. With years of experience in the classroom, teachers have seen what works and what doesn't work. Though they may be wary at first, as discussed earlier, once they see what is possible with serious games, they can become a source of ideas for new techniques and applications.

Quinn spoke a word of caution, however. "You can't just put game designers and educators in a room together," he said, and expect to get something good out of it. Both the designers and the educators need to learn to communicate with each other so that both sides are saying the same thing and understanding each other. Then, the focus needs to be on the learning goals and designing a game that meets those goals.

It helps that the upcoming generation of teachers will have played nearly as many video games as the upcoming generation of game developers. This will facilitate both a shared vocabulary and a shared understanding of the desired outcomes.

Referring to the results of the Apple Classrooms of Tomorrow (ACOT) program sponsored by Apple Computer from 1985 to 1998, Ferguson described the changing dynamic of teachers and students. The teachers, who linked their pedagogical style to the computer in the classroom and gave their students more latitude about how they used the computer, discovered that the students would mentor one another. This mentoring of students by students changed the way the students learned. Instead of having traditional lectures with passive students, the roles of students and teachers re-aligned.

With the advent of serious games, game developers are in a position to help teachers not only evolve and improve their methods of teaching, but also to simultaneously bring the benefits of automation and information technology into the classroom. For too long, the only impact the Information Age has had on the classroom is Scantron test scanning, grade tracking, and, recently, Internet access. As developers of serious games interact with educators and listen to those educators, real change is possible. The tools of making games, the hardware to run them, the skills of game designers, and the latest theories of education can come together like never before.

Fun in Games Case Study—Hidden Agenda Contest

Trivial Pursuit–style games, with excessive multiple-choice questions, are not wanted in the Hidden Agenda contest, an annual contest for high school and college students, at both the undergraduate and graduate levels, sponsored by the Liemandt Family Outreach and Education Initiative. The goal of the contest, which is the biggest project in the 25-year history of the foundation, is to create "stealth education," said Lauren Davis, Director of Stealth Education for the foundation, with students learning almost by accident as they play a game. "Stealth education," a phrase attributed to Doug Crockford of LucasArts, is learning that doesn't seem like learning or work because it is fun. The player learns while having fun.

Traditional learning, Davis added, works well for some students, but not others. There have been very few major changes in how school is taught in the last century. The Hidden Agenda contest hopes to provide new ways for students to learn while having fun.

Currently, the contest targets the middle school level, which is where Davis thinks the most good can be done. At that age (12 to 15 years old), Davis said, the students are at a stage in life where they are trying to get their bearings. They resist outside messages and have a tendency to push back at the structures of formal education. Also, the middle school educational market appeared underserved. While there is a host of material for preschoolers and children just learning to read, and there has been a lot of growth at the university level and corporate training for adults which can be used for high school students, according to Davis, there has been a dearth of options for middle schoolers.

One controversial criterion of the Hidden Agenda contest is that the entered games are judged 70 percent on their entertainment value and only 30 percent on their education value. The logic is that if a game is 90 percent education, students won't get past the first screen. Therefore, the contest emphasizes fun. The contest judges are middle school students as well as teachers, game designers, and professionals with experience in game-based learning. Games haven't seen widespread use in classrooms yet, Davis went on, because not only do the teachers not trust that the games are teaching the material well enough, but also because many of the games are not fun.

The foundation will do testing to make sure that the games are teaching the desired material, but they don't want that testing to get in the way of the player enjoying the game.

The contest is only open to students, currently, because the foundation likes the idea of getting new concepts from students who are still involved in the educational process. Also, Davis believes that it helps to have fresh ideas from people who haven't been steeped in the common practices of the video game industry. The team with the top entry is awarded a cash prize of $25,000. According to Davis, the Hidden Agenda contest produced five "phenomenal games" in its first year. The foundation's budget, unfortunately, allowed them to put only two of those into production. The first of these, she said, would be available by fall 2005.

Stealth education won't replace teachers, Davis insisted. Instead, it will provide an additional educational tool. For example, a teacher can provide a Hidden Agenda game to students either as homework or as a non-required way to reinforce the lessons in class. Playing on their own, the students learn from the game.

Davis said that, so far, they haven't run into any resistance from teachers. The teachers recognize that their students play games and would like to tap into some of that extra energy expenditure. The students, of course, are excited by the idea.

The foundation doesn't plan to sell the Hidden Agenda games in quantity to school systems. Instead, they plan to distribute the games via retail and directly to interested parents and teachers on the Web. While they don't expect to see mass usage of games in the classroom in the short term, Davis said, "a lot can be done school by school, kid by kid, to show that this is a valid way to teach and to learn."

Other marketing options include partnering with organizations like the Telecom Pioneers. The Telecom Pioneers is a charitable project, with a group of retired telecommunications professionals that teach middle school students about the telecommunications industry. Such organizations could buy those Hidden Agenda games that are relevant to them and then give them away to the students they talk to.

There are many different methods of distributing the games, Davis said. The key is that the game is going to be fun. When the game is fun, it will spread through grass roots and word of mouth.

Pitching Educational Games

In the United States, unlike many other countries, such as in Japan and France, the specifics of what are taught in the classroom are set at the local level and not at the national level. This local emphasis provides an opening for game developers who want to create serious games for education. They do not need to pitch to the entire nation. They can, instead, pitch to the local school board. This applies to all levels: grade schools, middle schools, high schools, colleges, and universities.

As we mentioned earlier, parents have become the primary target for most commercial educational games and software. Game developers who wish to sell directly to parents are essentially targeting the retail market. This can be a difficult market to penetrate without the backing of a publisher or other profit-motivated corporation. The alternative is to sell directly to the parents via the Web or become their own publisher and negotiate distribution deals with interested retailers.

Besides serving as the gatekeepers to the home educational software market, parents also exercise considerable control over what is taught and how it's taught at the schools their children attend. The local Board of Education and the Parent Teachers Association (PTA) are powerful organizations that set and influence policies at public schools. Parents who send their children to private schools tend to be even more involved with how the institution is run, how the curriculum is used, and how the philosophy of the teachers impacts their children.

When a school is already successful using traditional methods of education, it is less likely to consider alternative methodologies. Learn Technologies Interactive created *Archaeotype*, a game that simulated an archaeological dig of a 5th century BC Greek ruin and developed a number of similar products covering such subjects as astronomy and Shakespeare. Originally, these products were for a prestigious private high school in New York.

In the end, though, the school board lost interest in the products because they did not think they needed to change their pedagogy. The students were already getting into Ivy League schools, so the school board didn't see any reason to change.

Homeschooling, and the even more free-form education pursued by "unschoolers," could prove to be a significant market for serious games. Homeschooling parents are always on the lookout for new material and new ways to teach their children. Many of them subscribe to the same publications as professional teachers, but with the freedom to "cherry pick" the materials and lesson plans they want to use. Homeschoolers also tend to be part of cooperatives and, if one member of the group likes a particular product, they promote it to the group.

Unfortunately, despite their influence, parents, either as part of the Board of Education or other organization and as groups of individuals, seldom have access to the funding required by retail games. Thus developers will want to focus on smaller, less expensive productions.

As another alternative, Aldrich listed a number of foundations that have expressed an interest in education, such as the George Lucas Educational Foundation (GLEF), the Milken Family Foundation, and the Chewonki Foundation. The Liemandt Foundation, mentioned earlier in the "Hidden Agenda Contest" case study, is another such organization.

Development Issues

The primary development issues in serious games for education are the small budgets and the broad range of possible hardware and software to be supported. The need to work closely with educators, for their expertise and because they are a necessary part of the educational experience, has already been discussed at length.

Like most people outside the retail video game industry, a lot of teachers will have little to no information or experience with game development. Game developers will need to help them understand the process. They may have to explain what's possible and what's not, especially with the limited budgets available.

Small Budgets

In Chase's experience, retail video game publishers tend not to be interested in educational games. The publishers aren't interested in selling to a small market. They want to sell *millions* of copies. There just aren't enough teachers to command the attention of the publishers. Edutainment, which targets parents, a much larger market than teachers, has become a significant market, but it is still not enough to interest the big publishers.

On top of that, Chase found little interest from the big publishers for a game that simulated something so mundane as a national election. He spent a year trying to sell *Power Politics III*, but no publisher wanted an election game until the great excitement of election night 2000. Unfortunately, even then the attention was short-lived, and Kellogg Creek Software found itself developing the game on its own. As a long-time independent developer, though, Chase was up to the task. The difficulty faced by Chase and all independent game developers is that there is currently no established business model for making money doing it. "'Cheap' is more than most schools can afford," Chase said.

It's not just the independents struggling with selling their games, however. Prensky described the problem Lucas Learning had with their first title, *Droidworks*. How should the game be marketed? And where should retailers place it on their shelves? Does it belong with the other games or with similar education products? This confusion proved detrimental to sales.

Taken as a whole, the current conditions severely limit the amount of funding available for general education-oriented games. Even very willing organizations often have only a fraction of the typical video game budget available. Developers will need to be extremely cost conscious and focus on leveraging pre-existing and easily created content and resources.

Equipment

The range of computer systems in use in education is quite broad. There are desktops, laptops, and even handheld devices spanning several generations of software and hardware. An additional wrinkle is that the hardware won't always be versions of the same platform but could be a mix of old and new computers from Apple as well as Windows-based PCs. This puts an emphasis on supporting cross-platform development to reach the widest possible market.

Fortunately, this is becoming less of an issue as the cost of computers and software comes down and the lifespan of both continues to rise. Hardware and software are now regular budget items in school systems. Still, to reach the broadest possible audience, developers should target technology that is going to be generally available at the time they finish development.

The good news, according to Chase, is that serious games for the classroom don't have to have eye-popping, state-of-the-art graphics, especially "if you have something else to hook them." The continued success of retro games from the 1970s, 1980s, and early 1990s, where the graphics were seldom the main draw, shows that even today's youth enjoy a good game, even if it's not up to the latest 3D, real-time rendering standards.

Desktops and laptops are the primary platforms, currently, but Klopfer predicted that handheld personal digital assistants (PDAs) would become more popular in the future. Not only are PDAs less expensive, which is always an important feature for schools, but PDAs eliminate the need to move the students into a special computer lab. The teacher can simply hand out a PDA to each student and get on with the lesson.

Conclusion

Like video, film, and even books have done in the past, video games are becoming a part of the educational process. Video games offer a flexible, non-linear, learner- directed approach to learning that will become even more important in the globalization underway in the 21st century. No matter how important they become, though, serious games will not replace teachers, professors, and other educational facilitators. Instead, these games will be part of the new educational toolbox.

The evolution to new teaching paradigms that fully utilize video games is already underway. This evolution will only get faster as more and more of the so-called video game generation become teachers and professors.

There is a catch, though. The video game industry has always been profit-centered. Serious games for the military and other government agencies, as we discussed in Chapters 4 and 5, and for corporations, as we will discuss in the next chapter, come with a built-in funding system. The government has no problem providing the funds to improve the training of its troops or to stimulate research and development of new technologies. Similarly, businesses are willing to spend money to get a better return on their investments in training. Schools, however, especially public schools, seldom have the revenue or the necessary extra funding to invest in the development of new software.

New approaches to funding serious games for education will have to be discovered. Maybe the retail video game publishers will start earmarking funds to explore this new market, or maybe the future is in creative corporate sponsorships, such as those Kellogg Creek Software is forming for its games. Or maybe the money will come from a direction no one has yet considered. The future remains open.

Serious games for corporate training will be discussed in the next chapter.

7

CHAPTER

CORPORATE GAMES

Corporations have a wide variety of training needs and have shown an increased interest in using serious games in the workplace. Driven by rapid, global changes in technology and business practices, all employees, from the executive boardroom down through the ranks to the mailroom and stockroom, need to know more about their jobs and the tools of their trade than ever before.

Since the training needs of many companies tend to be similar, there are opportunities to offer training across the entire business spectrum. The corporate e-learning market in the United States is expected to exceed $10 billion by 2007. In addition, the percentage of e-learning products based on computer simulation is expected to reach 40 percent by 2008. The percentage is around 10 percent, currently. That's a big opportunity.

In this chapter, we will review the history of corporate training and the growth of the use of computers as a part of that training. We will also survey the breadth of possible serious games within the corporate arena, from strategic simulations for executives to sensitivity training for middle managers and supervisors to procedural training for employees. Finally, we will discuss some of the issues that must be faced when doing corporate serious games development.

GAMES AT WORK

Corporate training is an outgrowth of the expansion of large corporations over the past century and a half. As corporations grew, they began requiring more and more specialized training in equipment and procedures. Such narrow training was often outside the scope of college and university courses and degree programs. Therefore, corporations had to fill this need on their own.

Many companies built in-house training facilities, and some of these eventually spun off their training as a separate business venture. In other cases, companies were formed specifically to offer training for other companies. Today, corporate training is a multi-billion dollar industry. As we mentioned above, the market for corporate e-learning is estimated to reach $10.6 billion by 2007. This makes it a similar-sized market to that of entertainment video games, though not all of that money will be invested in serious games for training. Like traditional education, corporate training has adopted new media and technology as they have come available. Training films and printed manuals supplemented lectures, and then along came e-learning with the advent of computers and the Internet. Now, serious games offer a much more powerful way to educate, and corporations are adapting to their use in training programs.

Computers, the Internet, and E-Learning

In the early 1980s, computer-assisted training came into existence, taking its place alongside training films and videos, but it wasn't until the 1990s that major changes occurred, morphing computer-assisted training into e-learning. Multi-media PCs with their large capacity CD-ROMs, and later with access to the Internet and World Wide Web, enabled e-learning to eclipse traditional training methods.

E-learning courses on personal computers displaced training films, videos, and lectures for several reasons. Mostly, though, corporations embraced e-learning because it afforded them significant cost savings. Training staff could be reduced, as well as floor space and equipment devoted to training.

Further, template shells with customized content could be created quickly and distributed easily to employees. Tom Peters, in his book *Re-Imagine!*, reported that IBM in the last few years has moved most of its training activities out of the classroom and onto the desktop. As a result, IBM saved close to a quarter-billion dollars.

However, in a very real sense, e-learning was not so radical a change from the training videos it replaced. Rather than viewing VHS or Beta cartridges on a TV or projector, employees could instead find the videos burned onto laserdiscs or DVDs or more recently, streamed across the company's network to the employee's workstation. There, the employee watched the videos and read the material in much the same manner as before. At most, a Web-like interface would be created to manage the training steps and to provide simple, multiple-choice tests of the material covered.

Clark Aldrich, in his book *Simulations and the Future of Learning*, talked at length about e-learning and how it compares to more sophisticated training simulations. E-learning, he said, uses many of the same words that have become popular with serious games, such as "engaging" and "simulation." Despite this shared terminology, most simulations in e-learning are based on only linear branching or PowerPoint-style presentations. To Aldrich, this type of product is not a simulation, but rather a "simulation of a simulation." Aldrich noted that when the armed forces need mission-critical training, they use simulations, as in flight simulators and vehicle simulators, but not e-learning.

Furthermore, some skills, like personnel management and interpersonal skills, are not easily or well taught using the linear methods of e-learning. Trial and error, and the resulting accumulation of knowledge of what works and what doesn't, are not possible in simplistic e-learning products. To really learn, instead of simply memorizing answers, trainees need to be involved in what's being taught, to actively weigh consequences and mull over decisions. E-learning, a mostly passive exercise in which trainees need to absorb material through multiple-choice options, does not encourage that kind of thinking.

Despite the early enthusiasm for e-learning, it has not proven to be particularly engaging for trainees. Completion rates for online corporate training are less than 50 percent, even though online training is more freely available than ever before. After all, e-learning removed from corporate training the one part that employees liked: a chance to get out of the office.

In addition, just because someone finishes an e-learning course doesn't mean that they understood the topic or will remember the material over time. During a sexual harassment prevention course, for example, the trainees read the material and take the quizzes, often on the same day. As long as they score well enough on the quiz, they pass the course and are then expected to understand what is sexual harassment. But do they? And on the other side of the issue, how often do the companies even check to see that all of the material was read and understood?

Games and Gamers on the Clock

Corporations have become interested in serious games and simulations for a variety of reasons. More and more of their employees have grown up with video games. This makes them more receptive to learning from games and simulations and may even have made them better employees. Besides familiarity with the medium, though, the use of serious games could also result in significant cost savings and improvements in the effectiveness of corporate training.

Why Games (at) Work?

Marc Prensky, the founder and CEO of games2train.com, pointed out in his book, *Digital Game-Based Learning*, that a growing number of corporate employees come from the so-called "Video Game Generation." According to the 2004 Consumer Survey conducted by the Entertainment Software Association (ESA), the average age of a game purchaser is 36, which increases the likelihood these game players are part of the corporate ranks. Indeed, according to a survey of over 2500 American workers, John Beck and Stephen Wade reported in their book, *Got Game: How the Gamer Generation Is Reshaping Business Forever*, that 81 percent of those workers aged 34 or younger labeled themselves frequent or moderate gamers. For the video game generation, video games have been a part of their life since childhood. Films and books, or the "old way" of learning, hold less of an interest for them. As video game players become an increasing number of the workforce, it's conceivable that future generations will be even less interested in the old, static forms of learning.

To combat this disinterest in traditional corporate training, some corporations have turned to serious games. Serious games offer a way to engage the interest of the trainee quickly and effectively. Thus trainees get through training and into production faster, all at a lower cost than traditional methods.

Kevin Corti, Managing Director of PIXELearning, a United Kingdom–based company that creates games and simulations for corporate training and education, agreed. Flexibility and adaptability will be requirements for all businesses and their employees in the 21st century, and traditional training methods will not always be able to meet these objectives in a cost-effective way. Even e-learning, he insisted, at least in its current form, will be unable to deliver the "deep levels of learning experience" necessary. "As the gamer and digital generations continue to form an even larger proportion of the work force," he said, "[they] will increasingly demand learning opportunities that are delivered in the way that is appropriate to them."

Serious games also offer a significant paradigm shift in training. No longer will employees be presented with information that can be ignored. Instead, they are immersed in the lesson to be learned and are expected to demonstrate their mastery of the material within the context of the serious game.

Kathleen Iverson, in her book *E-learning Games: Interactive Learning Strategies for Digital Delivery*, referred to this as the changing role of the trainee from "passive vessel" to "active participant." Students have more interaction with this new training method. They interact with the material, with each other, and with the trainer. In a way, the trainee also becomes a teacher, via "peer learning," if there are other trainees participating in the course.

The role of the trainer also changes, Iverson said, from being a "sage on stage" to that of a "guide by the side," or facilitator. Prensky also saw the role of corporate trainers changing. Trainers will now be creating content, motivating the trainees to interact with the content, tutoring the trainees when they face difficulties, and debriefing them afterward to help them assess what they learned and put it in context.

Beyond building employee skills, there is interest in applying serious games in other ways. Van Collins, Studio Head at Offshore Safety Initiative (OSI), said they had received requests for serious games related to incident management and disaster preparation. Every time there's an oil spill or major accident, the investigating safety team at an oil company writes a detailed analysis of the incident. From this analysis comes new safety changes and recommendations. In addition to teaching safety skills, serious games could be used to simulate the incident to help in the analysis and also to review possible ramifications of new recommendations.

Gamers Clock In

In their book, *Got Game: How the Gamer Generation Is Reshaping Business Forever*, Beck and Wade talked at length about the advantages video game players bring to the corporate world and how those same video game players will help lead companies into the future. For example, gamers have a strong understanding of risk versus reward and are more likely than other groups (that is, non-gamers) to take measured risks. Gamers have learned that video games don't reward unnecessary risk, and thus gamers in business roles tend to take only those risks that are right for the business. Gamers have a natural competitive edge when it comes to dealing with trade-offs, an essential part of business.

Furthermore, Beck and Wade insisted, today's business climate, with its rapid change, global competition, and exploding complexity, will require employees with deep analysis skills. In this world of uncertainty, it's getting harder and harder to be make educated decisions about anything without complex analysis. The tools of the past, such as spreadsheets and linear models, are ineffectual against the onslaught of constant streams of available data. Gamers, with their multitasking skills, will warm to the more sophisticated analytical tools that may resemble video games.

This similarity to games can have unexpected or emergent results. In some cases, the use of serious games has resulted in trainees discovering more effective processes. For instance, during the 1991 Gulf War, the U.S. military noticed tank drivers and pilots using new strategies and tactics. When interviewed later about what they had done, the soldiers replied that they had employed the same methods in simulations during training. As corporations strive to streamline production pipelines and processes, this kind of emergent optimization will be valuable.

A Short History of Games at Work

In the early 1980s, one of the first video games designed for corporate training was developed: *Where in the World is Carmen Sandiego's Luggage*. The client, Scandinavian Airlines Systems, needed a customer service training tool, and the popular adventure game character seemed a perfect fit. Carmen Sandiego had lost her wallet, and the trainee was the customer service person she approached to help her find it. Developed with Hypercard for the black-and-white screens of the Apple Macintosh, *Where in the World is Carmen Sandiego's Luggage* proved to be the part of the training course that trainees liked most, said Prensky in a presentation at the 2005 Game Developers Conference.

A more recent example is the game *Objection!* by TransMedia. This game gives trial lawyers practice in the proper timing and procedures for objecting to opposing counsel's questions or comments. Originally written for MS-DOS, and then later updated for Windows, *Objection!* has expanded to be a series of games that cover various types of civil suits and witness testimony. The games have even been approved for Continuing Legal Education (CLE) credit in many of the United States.

Employees and lawyers haven't been the only audience for corporate training games. In 1998, Ameritrade created *Darwin: Survival of the Fittest*. The game teaches options trading by putting the player in the trading pit. Ameritrade offered the *Darwin: Survival of the Fittest* CD-ROM free to teach their customers. That same year, the company did an informal poll of people who had requested the game and played it. Fifty-one percent said that their knowledge of options was greater than it had been before they played the game.

Most companies today, Prensky said, have a serious game in use for training somewhere within the organization, even if it's only a variation on *Jeopardy!* Sony, who owns the *Jeopardy!* IP, has licensed *Classroom Jeopardy!*, a shell of the game for use by teachers and corporate trainers. Typically, such games are used by a particular trainer on an ad hoc basis and are not a part of the overall training system. However, he added, the use of serious games in corporate training is not yet commonplace. Overall, serious games have yet to permeate corporate training culture, but there are more and more of them coming into use each month.

Going Beyond E-Learning Case Study—PIXELearning

PIXELearning Limited, which has a background in e-learning, has been making serious games for training since 2002 but has evolved in several ways since its inception. First, the company shifted from being a "work for hire" contractor to a provider of technology products. At the same time, its products have evolved, from somewhat simplistic edutainment-type content to sophisticated business simulations. In response to these changes, the company has shifted its business focus from targeting the entire education and learning space to the narrower corporate training space, specifically business and management skills development.

E-learning, Corti said, has become defined primarily as Web-based learning content and delivery with an emphasis on delivering information, "which few would consider to be interactive." This type of delivery, Corti went on, has not proven successful at providing "rich, rewarding, relevant, and multi-faceted environments" where trainees can put into practice what they've been taught. In contrast, Corti described the medium of serious games as "highly self-motivational" because those are exactly the advantages provided.

Unlike e-learning, serious games offer the trainee a chance to gain experience in the subject being taught. Corti added, "As a wise man once said 'Experience is like giving a comb to a bald man . . . it often comes too late!'" To put it another way, he said, "Do you want your sales team to learn *about* sales or do you want them to know *how* to sell?"

PIXELearning believes in the power of serious games to train in a "very wide and diverse range of applications across all sectors, for many purposes, and on a global scale." They also believe in what Corti referred to as "authentic learning." Authentic learning makes training personally meaningful and relevant to the trainee by showing how the trainee will use the training in the real world. Authentic learning gives the trainee the "opportunity to think in the modes of the subject/discipline." Furthermore, PIXELearning strives to test the learner in situations much like those found in the real world rather than with simple multiple-choice questions.

Corti described the typical PIXELearning business simulation as drawing on role-playing game techniques. "Typically the user is responsible in-game for a company, department, or project where there is a predefined scenario and set learning objective." For Corti, serious games are "games for which the primary purpose is not entertainment but where entertainment serves to reinforce the learning experience."

When asked whether he thought game development companies might be able to move into the corporate training market, Corti expressed the opinion that experienced game developers may have an advantage over traditional e-learning companies in capitalizing on the opportunities of serious games. Even though serious games and e-learning may seem to be closely related, Corti remarked that "the design and development competencies of the e-learning developer and the game developer are quite different." Serious games, with their ability to create rich environments where trainees can put what they've been taught into practice, are far removed from the simple "click-to-continue the streamed video presentation" of most e-learning.

DEVELOPING GAMES FOR THE WORKPLACE

Now we shift our focus to some of the more significant differences from traditional, retail game development that game developers are likely to encounter when designing, pitching, and building serious games for corporate training.

To reiterate a point that has been made several times in this book: The main strength of game developers is their understanding of how to take training material and turn it into a fun playing experience, but there's more to the serious games equation than fun. Every industry has its own specific "domain knowledge" that will likely be far removed from what most game developers have had to learn. Thus developers should acknowledge the limits of their expertise and experience and seek out the help of experts in the corporate and corporate training worlds.

Design Issues

Just making a game, or a game-like product, out of the training material is not enough. Corporate trainers aren't the best game designers and may tackle the subject matter in too straightforward, or too obvious, a manner. In his book, Prensky talked about what he called the "typical customer service simulation." The customer, either animated CG or full-motion video, walks into the shop and has a simulated conversation with the trainee based on a dialog tree. There are different types of customers and different types of situations, all designed to illustrate the training points. If the trainee picks a wrong answer, he or she gets negative feedback from the customer and possibly an "expert opinion" on why the selected answer was incorrect. The problem with this type of product, according to Prensky, is that it feels like training. If the trainees were not forced to go through it, they wouldn't. In an effort to make an obligatory task fun, though, the trainees may choose the most outrageously wrong answers, just to see what might happen in the negative feedback.

Beck and Wade emphasized the need for training games to support trial and error. Game players have a strong disinclination to read manuals. Fortunately, gamers have an aptitude for electronic stories. They can read, of course, but they like to try things on their own and discover the necessary information.

Range of Topics

Corporate training covers much more than just company policies on customer service, call center etiquette, and any kind of sensitivity training.

Certainly, there are a lot of topics in common from one company to the next, but each business has its own specific training needs that match its market. This creates a wide range of possible training games, maybe even wider than many game developers are accustomed to considering.

Video games developed in the United States have a tendency to be action games with a focus on war and combat, sports, and other competitive pastimes. Corporations, though, at both ends of the size spectrum, need to train their employees in a wide variety of skills, and most of them aren't competition-based:

- **Job-specific skills**. How to use the hardware and software required by the job.

- **People skills**. How to work well within the team, department, and overall company.

- **Organization skills**. How to best organize their time and resources, or the time and resources they are responsible for.

- **Communication skills**. How to effectively present their ideas and feedback to their co-workers, superiors, and those under them, when speaking, writing, and so on.

- **Strategy skills**. How to set goals for the team, department, division, or company and how to leverage the available resources to reach those goals.

More specific examples of training needs include sexual harassment prevention, religious sensitivity, ethics, equipment safety, and so on. Prensky offered these additional suggestions for situations where game-based learning would be useful:

- When the material is dry, technical, and boring.

- When the subject matter or process is complex or particularly difficult to understand or transmit.

- When parts of the audience are hard to reach.

- When assessment and certification could be difficult using other methods.

- When performing sophisticated "what-if?" analysis.

- When developing or communicating corporate strategies.

Taken together, these lists present a very broad range of possible serious games. However, those lists focus on employee training. Corporations might have other types of training they want to do, such as customer training. More than the simple animated billboards of "advergaming," corporations that sell complex software or hardware are interested in training their customers how to get the most out of their product. This type of training game could also cover suggested uses for the product, which the player can explore and try out on their own.

Many serious games for the corporate market, like those for the military, will be highly accurate, open-ended simulations of real-world systems, vehicles, and situations. Others, though, can be more abstract, more akin to slow, thoughtful strategy games or puzzle games, with more latitude in how the information is presented and how the trainee interacts with that information. Even *Jeopardy!*-style games have their place. Just as in entertainment video game design, the only real limits are those the designer chooses. Almost anything is possible.

On the other hand, when designers choose their approach to serious games, Collins recommended they avoid the temptation to be too "lighthearted." Corporations, as a rule, tend to take themselves and what they do very seriously and may not show much of a sense of humor. Humor makes corporate training more bearable, but there's definitely a line that can't be crossed.

Measurable Results and Reporting

Measurable results are just as important in the corporate world as they are in the education arena. Since the results of the serious game can have an effect on the company's bottom line and, in some cases, potential liability, the company will be scrutinizing them carefully.

Large, multinational corporations, said Eric Marcoullier, Director of Serious Games at Cyberlore Studios, are "quant-focused" and demand proof of the effectiveness of training products. Marcoullier said he considered games to be great tools for assessment because "just about any event or state can be tracked and evaluated." For Cyberlore's future serious games products, the company plans to have extensive internal measurement components in order to track the trainee's true learning. In the meantime, Cyberlore integrates with the client's database system so that tests can be run to prove the efficacy of the training in the real world. The trainee is presented with a problem or situation that utilizes the company's accumulated data, and then observed to see how well he or she handles the situation compared to that data.

This is a key aspect of serious game development, Corti said. The serious game designer must know how to integrate effective and appropriate assessment methodologies into the learning experience. These methodologies must demonstrate skills competencies, and gaps in those competencies, to both the learner and the manager or mentor.

PIXELearning's products include pre-game, in-game, and post-game assessment, Corti said. Assessment within their games is both quantitative and qualitative, and allows "the game experience to adapt to the learner's performance, to give the learner the feedback that they need in order to understand the relationship between their actions/decisions and in-game outcomes." Also, "it provides the training manager with the detail that they need in order to accurately understand the extent of the learner's mastery of the subject." Further, Corti said that PIXELearning's game engines provide the training designer with the ability to create custom reports and filters.

Collins said that OSI's safety training simulation tracks such data as how long it takes the trainee to complete the lesson, the number of mistakes made, the number of self-corrections made, and more. For example, in the simulation of a helicopter platform (see Figure 7.1), the learner has a number of safety items available to give the team. If the learner gives the team hard hats, that would be a mistake because on a helicopter platform, a hard hat can become a lethal projectile. However, if, at the last minute, the learner takes away the hard hats, that would be a self-correction.

How the assessment is implemented depends on the nature of the game. A simple, multiple-choice question form should be considered the minimum level of assessment and not the most desirable. There are many forms of assessment. With a simple replay option, for example, trainers and trainees can review the exercise together. With more detailed logging and analysis of the information, additional feedback can be generated by the game and used for scoring, discussion, and further learning.

The importance of designing for assessment has been mentioned before, and it will be mentioned again because this is an issue that is frequently encountered in serious games. Awareness of the need for assessment from the beginning can reduce frustration for both the game developer and the company.

Figure 7.1

Offshore safety training

© OSI. Used with Permission

Equal Opportunity and Accessibility

Game developers have become increasingly aware of localization issues in the last decade. The ability to offer multiple languages and user interfaces has become important for marketing (and therefore selling) games in other countries. With serious games, though, especially in the corporate arena, localization of language and onscreen icons can be only a small part of what's necessary.

Employers in many nations, whether they are big multinational corporations or small mom-and-pop stores, have to be aware of equal opportunity laws and issues. Equal opportunity laws usually forbid discrimination or harassment of employees based on their race, gender, and religion. In addition, there is the need to support employees and customers who have disabilities.

The first set of issues, those dealing with discrimination and harassment, are primarily content issues. The design of the game should be sensitive to how race, gender, and religion are portrayed within the context of the game. In the same vein, the content of the training game should not be too tightly bound to a particular culture. When that happens, it's possible to make assumptions that would be offensive to or discriminate against trainees from a different culture. An example Prensky gave was gambling. In some cultures and even for some subgroups within the U.S., gambling is considered unacceptable and immoral.

On the other hand, simulations that are too politically correct can lose touch with the organization's actual culture and appear laughable. Almost like a Hollywood sitcom, the multicultural workplace that also gives the perfect work-life balance may appear to originate from la-la land. Even though that might be the public message that the company wants to project, the designer should focus on the training need rather than public relations.

To make the simulation more relevant to trainees, Prensky recommended asking for player input and preferences. In addition, he suggested that to ensure better participation of trainees of both sexes, the developer should design the game to support both competitive and cooperative modes. He listed four main factors in a diverse work force that could affect the success of the game:

- **Age.** Older workers tend to prefer traditional training tools, while younger workers prefer more interaction.

- **Gender.** The types of games preferred by males might be different from those preferred by females.

- **Competitiveness.** Some players delight in competitive games, while others prefer cooperative games.

- **Familiarity with games.** Not all corporate workers will be hardcore gamers. Those unfamiliar with games will need an intuitive interface. Avoid "combo moves" and "Easter eggs."

Prensky also recommended providing a non-game form of the information for those who don't like playing games—or just don't like the game as it is. Some people, after all, really do enjoying learning from books and videos and don't respond negatively to traditional tests.

In the United Kingdom, the Disability Discrimination Act (DDA) requires that training services be accessible to everyone. The United States Americans with Disabilities Act (ADA) makes similar provisions. The nature of games, requiring multiple senses (sight, sound, and touch, primarily), and use of complicated controllers, can make it a major, and possibly unobtainable, goal to achieve 100 percent compliance with these standards. Few available game engines have the necessary hooks to support alternative input and output devices, like screen readers for the visually impaired. But every effort should be made to make serious games as accessible as possible.

Like testing and assessment, these issues should be considered from the beginning of the design process.

The Element of Fun

Fun is the primary motivation for video game players, and game developers make this their main design goal. In serious games for training, however, fun is only useful as it gets the trainees to play the game and keeps them playing until they've learned the desired information, procedure, or technique.

It's important, Collins said, to keep in mind that the serious game is being designed with a training goal. OSI calls its serious games "games-based learning" solutions, and focuses on the accuracy of the simulation and compliance with the client's procedures and equipment. However, they still see the "game" part of the solution as important. With a game, the player is engaged. That's intrinsic to the product. With a training video, it's impossible to know if the trainee is sleeping in the back row. And even if the company gets a signed piece of paper, the company can't know for sure if the employee actually read a manual or understood the training.

At the 2004 Serious Games Summit in Washington, D.C., Paul Medcalf, Director of Multi-media for InSite Interactive, talked about the "trinity" of serious games design for corporate training: how to merge subject matter, instructional design, and game design ("making it fun"). To integrate games with training, Medcalf discussed using games to build momentum, to generate enthusiasm among trainees. He also talked about using games to measure retention of the material presented and using games for instruction via simulated situations.

"A game's success," Andrew Kimball, CEO of QBInternational, said at the same panel discussion, "is directly related to the learner's motivation" to play the game. To provide that motivation, he recommended using both "intrinsic" and "extrinsic" rewards. Intrinsic rewards come from within, and the examples he gave were certificates of completion or achievement given to the learners when they mastered the game. Extrinsic, or external, rewards are in relation to other players through competition or rankings. The game should provide both types of motivation, if possible.

Iverson described the ARCS Model of Motivation, created by J. M. Keller, which could be used as a template for designing training games. This model provides a framework for generating motivation in trainees. ARCS is an acronym for attention, relevance, confidence, and satisfaction. Using attention-getting techniques, information relevant to the trainee is presented. As the trainee goes through the program and experiments with the information and techniques, the trainee's confidence grows and leads to satisfaction, a positive reinforcement of what was learned.

Prensky included the following checklist in his book for the design of serious games:

- Is the game fun enough that its appeal extends beyond the target audience? Would other people want to play it (and learn from it)?

- Is the game experience addictive, prompting players to play again until they master it?

- When people play the game, do they think of themselves as trainees or students? Or do they think of themselves as players?

- Does the game encourage the player to reflect on what's been learned?

It's interesting to note how the emphasis is placed on fun first, and then learning. To Prensky, if the game isn't fun, then it hasn't fully capitalized on the advantages serious games have over e-learning.

Pitching

Collins, who is also the founder of V3 Entertainment and has 15 years experience in retail entertainment games, saw a lot of similarities in the processes and technology used for both entertainment games and serious games, including pitching. Even further, in his estimation, OSI had a competitive edge because of his overlapping expertise. OSI attempts to exploit this edge in its presentations to potential clients.

Actively pitching serious games to corporations is necessary, said Collins, because in most cases the companies are not seeking out this type of training solution. The manuals, books, training films, and videos are what the executives and managers are familiar with, and these are what they look at first. Developers who want to make and sell serious games must be on the lookout for companies that might be searching for new training solutions. With this knowledge in hand, developers must be prepared to give those decision makers a presentation on why serious games are a good solution and why the developers should be hired to provide them.

Fortunately, experienced game developers are already accustomed to the need to pitch their games, so this shouldn't be too big of a shift for them. However, when it comes time to close the sale, Corti advised that the developer swap the words "game" and "fun" for "simulation" and "engagement" to make the result sound more familiar to corporate ears.

Companies in every conceivable industry have already used serious games in one form or the other, so developers should be open to moving outside the technology sector. In his book, Prensky listed examples of serious games used by airlines, auditing firms, automobile manufacturers, banks, beverage makers and bottlers, consultants, engine sellers, fast food restaurants, financial services companies, hotels, insurance companies, investment banking firms, logging companies, and tax preparers, among others.

The Bottom Line

As always, when pitching a product, the developer should make the needs of the corporation the main focus of the presentation. The most obvious need of a corporation is revenue, and the most obvious way to get their attention is by showing how their investment in serious games as training tools will save—or better yet, *make*—them money.

Kamau High, in his article "How Playing Power Drives Lessons Home" for the September 8, 2004 issue of *Financial Times*, listed three important areas of savings from serious games. First, there are cost advantages. With a training simulation, the company pays for the initial development cost, and then the main cost is over. Once built, many people can use the training simulation, making the cost per employee trained less and shrinking over time. This could even result in needing a smaller training staff or less reliance on outside trainers.

An additional cost savings, for multinational companies that need to train people around the world, is that using a training simulation involves no travel costs. The simulation can be used by employees wherever they are, on their own workstations, via the company's LAN or WAN. This can help reduce or eliminate the need to allocate valuable floor space to a training facility. Even companies that do not have people around the world, though, can benefit from having their people do the training from their house or cubicle.

Finally, training simulations can be customized for different groups. With the appropriate tools included, simulations can be tweaked and adjusted based on the needs of a particular department within the corporation. These changes are minor compared to the original cost, so again, this provides a cost saving.

Prensky, however, advocated focusing less on straight return on investment (ROI) or savings and more on strategic issues. He called saving money a "middle management argument," and middle managers don't control the big bucks. To get the approval for larger budgets, developers must show how their serious games will help corporations reach strategic goals and assist them in gaining and keeping an edge over their competitors. Alternatively, the developers could show how the serious games will prevent such strategic problems as regulatory violations or lawsuits from customers or employees.

Either approach is essentially targeting the bottom line, though the first is more about the short term, while the other looks to the future and long-term objectives.

Who to Talk to

Independent game developers are used to talking to publishers, said Clark Quinn, author of *Engaging Learning: Designing e-Learning Simulation Games*, and publishers are an audience that wants and needs games. Approaching corporations is very different, not the least because they don't usually think in terms of games, to want them or to need them. For that reason, Quinn suggested starting at the top level in the corporation, targeting someone who controls purse strings, and convincing them of the value of serious games. Starting at a lower level, even if the contact has a real need and wants to use serious games, puts the developer through the long, arduous corporate purchase cycle.

"You need to find somebody who has the vision," Quinn said. That's someone in the company who has a need and understands the new opportunity represented by serious games. This champion should have budget control or access to a higher- level executive who does have budget control. Those are the three main ingredients, he said: a specific training need, recognition of the power of serious games to meet that need, and the ability to provide funding.

So to whom should developers pitch at corporations? Not the chief technology officer, according to both Prensky and Collins. Instead, talk to the person who is responsible for training. Ideally, talk to somebody with responsibility for or control over the training budget. Such gatekeepers include training managers in the Human Resources department, or line managers. Neither of these may have budget control but both are crucial to the daily operations of the company, especially the line manager, and can say, "Yes, I need this."

Though it might seem the obvious place to start, the Information Technology (IT) department actually is not, and should be avoided, at least to begin with. "We usually don't like the IT department to be involved in the decision of whether or not to invest in our product," Collins said. Why? Because IT tends to be suspicious of anything that didn't originate with them and protective of the computers, network, and other infrastructure that the serious game project will use. The IT department is crucial later on, of course, because the serious game needs to integrate with the company's databases and so on. Once the project is approved, Collins added, IT is more cooperative.

OSI leverages its accumulated contacts, Collins said, to get referrals to meet with the appropriate corporate executive. The company tries to target the person who would be signing off on the contract. From there, they get passed down to the group or department responsible for safety, and then make their way back up the corporate hierarchy again to close the deal.

Prensky stressed that developers shouldn't consider corporate America as a homogenous group. There are some individuals, companies, and industries that are more receptive and some that aren't. If a company doesn't seem to be receptive, developers shouldn't spend too much of their time trying to win the executives over.

Even a company that is receptive to the idea of serious games for training will not be unanimous in its support for serious games. Not everyone at the executive level, nor in every department, is going to buy into the change.

Just as in education, where teachers have long considered video games the enemy of learning, corporations have a distrust of people having fun while on the clock.

As a rule, corporations do not want their employees to be playing video games. Some companies restrict video game sites from being accessed using the company's Internet connection, and other companies prohibit the playing of video games during working hours. Video games, in other words, are seen to hurt productivity.

Those of us old enough to remember will recall that the earliest IBM PCs didn't even support color monitors because color was considered unnecessary for business. Three decades later, that misconception has been almost entirely done away with, but there is still a negative perception about games in many companies. Developers pitching training games to corporations must be aware of this resistance and take steps in their presentation to answer the skeptics and overcome any objections.

Other Pitching Options

The Fortune 100 is a favorite pitching target, for an obvious reason: They have the money for the big budgets. However, even small companies have training needs. For instance, nearly half of all the sexual discrimination charges filed with the Equal Employment Opportunity Commission in 2004 were against companies with 200 or fewer employees. In the United States, federal antidiscrimination laws apply to businesses with 15 or more employees, but state or local statutes can affect even smaller companies. Though smaller companies may not individually have the funds for a significant budget, as a group, they can be a significant market.

According to Corti, PIXELearning doesn't limit itself to only the big companies, and they try to customize their approach to the size and direction of the company. "We believe that for serious games to have true value to an organization, they will need to reflect that organization's particular characteristics, be that language, industry sector, geographic location, ethos, ambitions, problems and/or drivers." Though PIXELearning has to create a number of client-specific solutions, primarily in the public sector, its focus is on developing a proprietary technology tool set that can be used to create solutions tailored to the specific company.

Corporate universities are another possible market for serious games. McDonald's has Hamburger University, JPMorgan Chase has the Executive Learning Center, Motorola has Motorola University, and more. These organizations exist for the sole purpose of training the corporations' executives, managers, and employees and are staffed much like regular universities. Unlike regular universities, however, corporate universities have access to the corporation's revenue stream and aren't dependent on government grants, endowments, and so on.

The public sector is also a possibility. Corti said that PIXELearning acquired grant funding from several sources to develop their initial technology, as well as funding the company through finding their first clients. In some cases, this funding came because the government was interested in economic development, particularly the creation of new jobs. Right now, Corti said, in the UK the "most revenue potential is from publicly funded sources." He expected that to change over the next few years, though, and he also expected the scope and scale of serious games training solutions to expand as the corporate world begins to see the bottom-line results it can achieve with the medium.

Contract Issues

Finally, moving from pitch to contract is often the longest part of the project and can be a challenge, unless the developer is talking to someone with the authority to allocate the budget or otherwise give the project the go-ahead. The time frame for going from pitch to signed contract can be as long, or longer, than game developers are accustomed to with retail publishers. Collins said that it took 24 months for OSI to pitch, negotiate, and sign its current contract. This kind of time frame requires the developer to keep a low burn rate or have sufficient funding to continue through the process.

Game developers used to retail publisher contracts will find both similarities and differences. One big difference is that the corporations are not as interested in owning the resulting intellectual property. Some will be, but many are more interested in using the product than owning it. We will discuss the importance of ownership of the final product, or at least the tools and source code infrastructure that supports it, later in this chapter. Other contract issues that companies might bring up include

- Payment terms

- Liability

- Publicity

- Use of the company name

When the developer gets paid is very important. Many companies, Prensky said, will try to get the developer to agree to doing the work first, and then being paid. The developer can, however, ask for, and usually get, a milestone-based payment schedule, as they are accustomed to in video game development. The important thing is to ask. Along with payment terms is the approval process by which the work done is accepted, and the payment is authorized. The developer should try to keep the approval process as fast and simple as possible, and requiring the signatures of the fewest number of people to avoid having the team sit idle between milestones.

Because the total payment for the contract is almost always going to be a fixed amount, the developer should be certain of the time and resources required for the project. If the developer overruns the agreed cost, they will almost always "eat" the extra, and the client will still demand the finished product at the agreed time.

Liability issues should be limited as much as possible, with the developer liable only for the software being built as agreed on.

Publicity and use of the company name should be agreed upon in writing. The developer should be able to trade on the work they've done, including listing clients they've worked for. If the client insists that their name not be used, there should be some form of compensation.

"People ask for a lot," Prensky said. But just because they ask for it, doesn't mean you have to give it to them. Almost everything is negotiable. An example he gave was companies asking the developer to create a pilot, or prototype, of the serious game unpaid. Since the pilot will almost certainly be a lot of work, the developer should insist on being paid at least some amount up front.

As in the entertainment games arena, sometimes, because of all the stipulations, restrictions, and requirements that a company is asking for, the best option may be not to sign any contract at all. No contract is almost always better than a bad contract.

Ultimately, "contracts are contracts," Marcoullier said, "and you're going to see the same clauses whether you're dealing with Electronic Arts, Cisco, Burger King, or the U.S. Government. Invest in an experienced lawyer who will watch your back."

Entertainment to Training Case Study—Cyberlore Studios

Based in Northampton, Massachusetts, Cyberlore Studios has been creating video games since 1992, releasing its latest game, *Playboy: The Mansion*, in early 2005. This long history in retail video games, and the proven ability to create immersive and engaging environments, is one of Cyberlore's "biggest competitive advantages," said Eric Marcoullier, Director of Serious Games for the company. "Cyberlore would not have landed our current serious games contract without our previous success developing games for retail."

"Training professionals," Marcoullier went on, "are now realizing they need to keep the new workforce involved in learning." Serious games offer a way for corporations to provide training in a way that their employees can connect with and understand and maybe even enjoy. "At the end of the day," he said, "the [trainee] has to *want* the training, and I don't know that it matters . . . whether that desire exists because the training is fun or just immersive. Regardless, game developers have a huge competitive advantage when it comes to creating engaging experiences."

So what prompted Cyberlore, a successful retail video game developer, to look into serious games? According to Marcoullier, there were two primary reasons. "First, there was a tremendous fit with our game technology," Marcoullier said. "Cyberlore is focusing on social [simulations] as an entertainment company, and there is a great opportunity for us to leverage that style of gameplay in the learning space." In particular, the engine created for *Playboy: The Mansion* provided a platform for simulating a wide variety of social situations.

Second, he said, serious games looked to be a way to bring in additional revenue for the company. Cyberlore, like all independent video game developers, faces the situation of surviving between publisher-funded projects described in Chapter 1. With its serious game projects, Cyberlore can have money coming in during the off times between retail projects.

Also, Marcoullier said, "with serious games, there is the potential to move from 'work for hire' to a 'product based' focus." With royalties from retail games getting scarcer and scarcer, especially for independent studios, the money such a studio can make can be estimated "by counting their billable employees." In other words, the company can expect little, if any, money after the publisher's advance payments. "If we are successful in creating a serious games training platform, then we'll move from selling manpower to selling products, and the upside potential is enormous." A billable man-hour, he pointed out, can only be sold once, but a product owned by the company can be sold over and over.

One more reason serious games appealed to Cyberlore is that with serious games "there's an opportunity to do something really meaningful." Though the company is focusing on training games for the near future, because of the current market potential, Marcoullier expressed an interest in other types of serious games, particularly healthcare and education. "I love the idea that the work we do may someday save lives or keep kids interested in learning all the way through their education."

Currently, Cyberlore has a single serious game project for a Fortune 100 client. This project, according to Marcoullier, is keeping about half the company busy, and the engine development and content pipelines are very similar to what they used in *Playboy: The Mansion*. The team is working closely with the client's training group, who is helping to create all of the training material in the game.

As of this writing, the project has been underway nearly nine months. Marcoullier figured Cyberlore could be working with the client on this training application for several more years and creating other training applications for them in that time. "As we get our generic training platform built," Marcoullier said, "we'll be able to create similar training games with far fewer resources."

With its software, Cyberlore can model complex relationships and social situations, allowing trainees to face circumstances and events they are likely to encounter in their work, make choices, and then see the consequences of their choices. Cyberlore has narrowed its focus to markets that involve a high degree of interpersonal interaction and customer service. Even with that focus, Marcoullier saw potential for the Cyberlore technology to be used in training for sales, nursing, casinos, prisons, and more.

Cyberlore's business plan for its serious games is to first target Fortune 1000 companies, and then the Global 5000 companies. "The scope of the training games we are creating requires that our clients have multi-million dollar training budgets." The company would like to move into shrink-wrapped retail, or even low-cost customizing, with its serious games. However, for the near future, Marcoullier sees Cyberlore's best chance for success with extremely large companies.

When asked if he saw serious games as a good option for other retail game development companies, Marcoullier said he did, but not for all of them. The history of the games industry, he said, is "littered with examples of companies searching for the Next Big Thing" and "I have a feeling that a lot of companies are going to look to serious games as a life raft." He didn't think serious games would be a good shift for some struggling entertainment companies because "all the things we struggle with as games developers (scheduling, client service, focus) are still here [in serious games], but the clients are much more complex and a lot less savvy." For those companies that have proven they can survive and succeed in the retail video game space, "this is a great opportunity to branch out and be successful in another area."

Development Issues

As we have mentioned in previous chapters, it's important for game developers to remember that the companies and learning professionals they are working with in the serious games space might have little or no experience with the process of designing and developing games. Corti stressed the need to manage expectations. It's not uncommon, he said, for uninitiated clients to expect a serious game with production values similar to AAA titles available at retail, but for "1 percent of the budget" of such titles. Also, they may have very strong opinions about the look of the resulting game, and especially how it works.

To prevent these types of issues from stopping the project, game developers will have to work at managing client expectations and educating the clients about the process—and when major changes to core features are no longer advisable. The clients don't always understand that adding features or increasing the level of simulation detail will take more time, Collins said, and the developer needs to be prepared to deal this.

Working with Corporations

A big difference with corporate clients, as opposed to retail game publishers, is that the companies are *clients*. This is a different relationship than the typical game developer-publisher relationship. "Working with large companies," Marcoullier said, "is far more complex than [working with] publishers." In addition to having to deal with more stakeholders and decision makers, Marcoullier said, "a significant amount of my time is spent just maintaining the client relationship."

A big part of this different relationship is the possibility for ongoing maintenance and modifications to the product. For serious games with a large scope, the development costs are only a small part of the total possible revenue. Corporations are used to signing multiyear maintenance contracts that accompany significant new software systems, and developers should consider taking advantage of this expectation to create new revenue streams.

Experienced game developers already know to keep the publisher, and increasingly, the licensor, involved in the process of development, but when dealing with a large company, the number of interested parties can be much larger. "I regularly interface with a dozen different people at the client," Marcoullier said, "and that will only increase as other divisions within the company become involved in the project."

Prensky offered the following list of issues that frustrate contractors working with companies:

- Getting a final decision, on anything, takes forever.
- Getting the appropriate signatures to accept a milestone and release payment is next to impossible.
- The list of features requested grows, while the budget stays fixed.
- Personnel changes within the company require forging new relationships.
- The developer can lose its independence working for a single large client.
- The client has ideas of its own and rejects those of the developer.
- The client wants worldwide support, all day, every day, with less than a five-minute wait.
- "Contracts take forever and corporate lawyers want too much."

Many of those will sound familiar to experienced game developers, of course. On the other hand, corporations have the following gripes about developers:

- The developer isn't flexible enough and doesn't want to respond to changing needs.
- Developers want everything in writing and charge for every little change.
- The developers want to "own and reuse," while the companies want work for hire.

Ultimately, Marcoullier said, "Making a game is making a game."

Possible Budgets

Prensky identified four levels of budgets, which correspond to levels of interest in serious games for corporate training. At the bottom are those companies looking to spend $10,000 or less on a serious game. At this level, the developer should consider basing the project on existing technologies and resources and avoid extensive development time or new content.

The real money only begins with the upper five-digit and six-digit budgets. At this level, Prensky said, you typically find sales departments and agencies that have a solid information technology infrastructure and healthy profit margins. At the final level, the training involves corporate strategy, with an impact on the company's bottom line stretching into the future. At this level, possible budgets can run into the millions, with the projects lasting at least a year.

Collins agreed. Most of the corporate projects he had seen were around $50,000 for a small implementation, or modification of a pre-existing game, ranging up to $1 million and beyond. For the larger projects, the companies brand it with their name and logo and provide detailed industry data, down to equipment size and performance specifications, and more. OSI targets Fortune 100 companies, specifically, the big oil companies. OSI has looked into smaller companies, Collins said, but for the near future, since OSI is still new, it has limited its involvement in serious games to only big projects (at the time of this writing, there were two in development) with big budgets.

Similarly, PIXELearning reported that projects built with its internally developed "BizSim" engine have ranged from £10k to £100k ($18,000 to $180,000 US)and last from three weeks to ten months with a team size of eight and a few freelancers. "We have won work through [submitting a bid]," Corti said, "but [we] were in a strong position to achieve this by virtue of being in on the projects from the outset and by helping to shape the tender/specification."

Corporate Hardware

Larger corporations usually have procedures in place to periodically update the hardware and software used by their employees. However, in many cases, the newest, most up-to-date computers tend to go first to the executives and managers, and then to the supervisors and, finally, to the rank and file. Even if a less hierarchical approach is used, computers are often kept in service as long as they continue to run properly. Thus it's not uncommon to find computers ranging from brand new to five or even 10 years old. So developers should be prepared to make their serious game work on a wide variety of possible hardware and software platforms.

Also, the cooperation of the company's IT department is crucial to deployment of the game. Though developers may want to avoid IT during the initial pitching process, IT is vitally important during development and deployment. The company's network, databases, and so on are usually the domain of IT, and the staff is very protective of those resources. And when it comes to games, IT is more accustomed to hunting down and ferreting out the video games employees have installed and deleting them. With the explosion of software viruses and e-mail worms, IT is more paranoid than ever. IT workers are not interested in any new software that will require a lot of additional bandwidth on the network or will make their jobs harder by introducing bugs and incompatibilities.

On the flip side, game developers often push the envelope of performance with their games because most of the time the game is the only software running on the computer. In the business world, this will not be the case.

For those reasons, developers should be prepared to work closely with IT, assuring that the delivered serious games will peacefully co-exist with the other software installed and running on the computer, such as monitoring programs and database front-ends, and play well with the other computers on the company network.

Build for the Future

Developers should always have an eye for how they can reuse the work they do on serious games for future projects. While the corporation will own many of the graphic resources and much of the other content they provided as the basis for the serious game, the game engine, will, with proper planning, be available for other projects for other clients. This includes the typical game engines, such as graphics rendering and networking, and also serious game-specific features, like the tools for creating lessons, the assessment engine, and more. "Typically," Corti said, "we developed the client's solutions at cost and retained title of the technology."

Prensky agreed, indicating that the first serious game project ought to be used for research and development to figure out what works and what doesn't, and so on. Then, the developer can take what's been done and turn it into a "template" for doing similar projects in the future. He advised developers to avoid signing any contract that prevents this business model. Or, if the company insists, use that point as leverage to greatly increase how much the developer will be paid for the project. Typically, though, unless the company is looking to market its own line of training games, it is unlikely to be interested in owning the resulting technology.

Businesses and business practices are always changing. Some training will require frequent updates to incorporate new information, new techniques, and so on. This is another reason developers should focus on the core parts of the serious game. Beyond making it possible to create additional games for other clients, it helps improve the profit margin on the maintenance contracts. To that end, Prensky advised keeping the content of the game external to the engine so that it can be updated quickly. The more tightly integrated the content and engine are, the more effort is required to change even one aspect of the game.

CONCLUSION

Compared to some of the other markets we've looked at, like the military and education, the use of games in corporate training is a relatively new development. Despite that, serious games have already become a widely used tool, and their use is only going to expand.

As Prensky pointed out, games are good for two things. First, there are particular techniques or attributes of games that can help people learn complex material faster and understand that material better. Second, games can increase the level of engagement of the trainees so that they want to play the game and they want to learn how to successfully complete the game.

Not all subjects and training objectives lend themselves to being taught in games, but where possible, and where those games manage to combine these two benefits, those games will be the most successful. That is what retail entertainment video game developers have to offer to corporate training.

In the next chapter, we will look at the use of serious games in a very serious environment: healthcare.

8

CHAPTER

HEALTHCARE GAMES

Video games are one of several sources for what the healthcare industry calls "repetitive stress injuries," or RSI. RSIs are injuries caused by putting stress on a joint in the same way, over and over again. Muscles and tendons around the joint become irritated and then inflamed as the body reacts to alleviate the stress. Common RSIs associated with video games are carpal tunnel syndrome and tendonitis. As most game developers are also avid game players, they are probably familiar with RSIs from first-hand experience (pun intended).

In the mental health arena, video games have been the subject of studies seeking to find a connection between gameplaying and aggression. This has proven to be a contentious topic, with implications at the national level. Lawmakers and advocacy groups have both made claims and counter-claims and sought restrictions.

But what if video games could actually improve the player's health? Modern medicine, both biological and psychological, has begun to take a deeper look at video games, looking past the RSIs and the politics to see the potential for healing. New studies have shown that video games can assist patients as they recover, help doctors as they prepare for delicate surgery, promote general wellness, help patients with mental problems, and more.

In this chapter, we will review how hospitals and mental health professionals have utilized video games in both treatment and training and how they hope to use video games in the future. We will also review how related not-for-profit organizations have used video games. Finally, we will cover the specific issues that face developers looking to design and sell serious games for healthcare.

GAMES FOR PHYSICAL AND MENTAL HEALTH

Healthcare professionals are looking to utilize the educational benefits of video games. A number of serious games now exist that target healthcare and well-being, like the "exergaming" game, *Yourself!Fitness*, and the biofeedback game, *The Wild Divine Project*, which combines breathing techniques and meditation with biofeedback. These new genres are recent developments.

More importantly, there has been an increase in the amount of research done in this area. In some of the research, games are used to probe the nature of the patient's condition. In other studies, the games are used therapeutically. Studies based on outcome research have always found positive implications of using games.

Dr. Mark Wiederhold, co-founder of the Virtual Reality Medical Center, talked about the many uses of video games (which he equated with "virtual reality") in modern medicine during his presentation, "The Potential of Games in Healthcare," at the 2004 Serious Games Summit in Washington, D.C. Some examples he gave were

- Using video games to distract patients during painful medical procedures.

- Using simulations to improve rehabilitation.

- Using virtual reality (VR) environments to improve motor skills.

- Using video games for therapeutic interventions.

Dr. Wiederhold's presentation focused on the use of inexpensive, off-the-shelf software and equipment. Especially inexpensive. "If it's not inexpensive, it won't be used," he stated. Some games are less suitable to healthcare purposes, but others have been surprisingly effective. He talked about using first-person shooter (FPS) games to treat fear spiders, since shooting seems effective in that case, but he added that he would like to move past that to gameplay mechanics that offered more depth.

Japanese game companies have paved the way for wider mainstream acceptance of serious games with healthcare benefits. Namco has created "rehabilitainment" products, also called "games for elders," and in 1999, entered the nursing home business. Konami, which acquired a fitness club franchise in 2001, expanded its brand with Konami Sports Club and Self Fitness Club and has been instrumental in merging fitness with entertainment. Similarly, Taito is moving into "amusement training." Unfortunately, in the U.S., healthcare games have largely been developed by independents, nonprofits, healthcare professionals, or concerned parents.

Hospitals and Medicine

Hospitals and larger clinics, often partnering with non-profit organizations and research facilities, have begun to experiment with alternatives to traditional treatments and therapies. Among their experiments have been a growing number that attempt to integrate video games into the treatment and recovery process. Video games have been used to distract patients during painful medical procedures as well as to improve motor skills in physical therapy and to speed recovery for certain operations and conditions.

On the other side of the treatment equation, doctors and other healthcare professionals are beginning to use video games as training tools. The advantages of being able to practice delicate surgery or dangerous procedures without having to actually perform the surgery or procedure on a living person are obvious.

Distraction Therapy

How much pain a person experiences often depends on how much conscious attention the person gives to the pain signals. Video games and virtual reality (VR), with their ability to immerse the individual in a computer-generated environment, have been shown to be effective in focusing a patient's attention away from their medical treatment and the pain they are experiencing. Immersed in the world of the game, they are not as consciously aware of what is going on around them, and they miss a proportion of the pain signals.

The Believe In Tomorrow Foundation, an organization founded in 1982 with the goal of improving the quality of life for critically ill children, has long been an advocate of the use of virtual reality or computer games for pain management. The foundation's Management and Distraction Technology program uses distraction as a pain management technique and has been employed in hospitals nationwide for almost two decades. Participating doctors and hospitals give children kaleidoscopes, squeeze balls, hand-held video games, and so on, before and after treatment. This teaches children an important key to enduring pain: Don't focus on the painful stimuli. The squeeze ball or the video game gives them something else to focus on and think about. Video games, particularly those with virtual reality (VR) immersion via headsets or similar technology, are a recent extension of that program.

The distraction is important before the treatment or procedure as well. Everyone is anxious before surgery and most other medical procedures. This is called *anticipatory anxiety*. Children seem to feel anticipatory anxiety more deeply than adults, to the extent that sometimes children need to be held down even for a simple injection with a hypodermic needle. The same distraction techniques can be used to alleviate anticipatory anxiety.

The Believe In Tomorrow Foundation found that developing games on its own, or contracting with experienced game developers, was cost-prohibitive. The immense budgets of modern games were beyond the foundation's non-profit, donation-funded means. Thus the foundation sought partnerships, such as the one with BreakAway Games. BreakAway Games, intent on showcasing the effectiveness of its serious games products, donated its deep sea diving simulator for use by the foundation.

In the summer of 2005, the Believe In Tomorrow Foundation will be conducting a new study in the effectiveness of VR techniques. Specifically, the study will compare a patient's pain tolerance when playing a video game to that when interacting in a VR environment. The goal of the study is to show that immersive VR is even more effective than playing normal video games, either handheld or on a console with a TV.

Self-Management

A key element in the treatment of chronic diseases, such as asthma and diabetes, is self-management. It is imperative that the patients adjust their lifestyle and habits to deal with the disease. The consequences of ignoring chronic conditions could be increased health problems or even death.

In 2000, *Patient Education & Counseling* reported on *Watch, Discover, Think, and Act*, a computer game designed to enhance self-management skills and improve asthma outcomes in inner-city children with asthma. Children ages six to seventeen years old from four pediatric practices were selected and randomly assigned to either use the computer game or the usual asthma education and treatment. The game's protagonist's asthma condition was tailored to match those of the child's, and, at the child's choice, the main character in the game could also be made to match their own gender and ethnicity. The children played the computer game as part of their regular asthma visits. The study found that the treatment associated with the computer game resulted in "fewer hospitalizations, better symptom scores, increased functional status, greater knowledge of asthma management, and better child self-management behavior."

In the same vein, *Packie & Marlon*, by ClickHealth, was designed to help children and teenagers with diabetes improve their diabetes self-management. The game, originally released for the Nintendo SNES and Windows 95, saw use at home, in hospitals, in clinic waiting rooms, and in diabetes summer camps. In a clinical study performed with the National Institutes of Health, ClickHealth found that children who played *Packie & Marlon* showed gains in self-efficacy, communication with parents, and diabetes self-care. They also had fewer urgent doctor visits for diabetes-related problems. More recently, in early 2005, Guidance Interactive Healthcare released *Glucoboy*, a glucose meter that can be connected to a Nintendo GameBoy. As a reward for maintaining good blood sugar control, *Glucoboy* downloads video game programs into the GameBoy.

Health Education and Physical Fitness

Other games try to help healthy players stay healthy. These games teach the players about topics like nutrition, physical fitness, and sexually transmitted diseases. Beyond just providing information, the games also try to promote changes in the player's behavior and future choices: to eat better, to exercise more, and to practice safe sex.

Using a video game, *Squire's Quest*, and related take-home assignments, researchers at Baylor College of Medicine reported improvements in the diets of Houston-area fourth-graders. *Squire's Quest* is a medieval-themed game where the player is a squire seeking to become a full knight. The player's knowledge of the nutritional content of different foods is tested as he designs healthy meals for King Cornwell and the royal family in a virtual kitchen and battles a variety of vegetable-destroying enemies. After five weeks of playing the game about 40 minutes per week during class, the nearly 800 students who participated in the program increased their fruit and vegetable intake by one serving a day on average.

Video games can also promote other healthy habits. Education has "edutainment," and now physical fitness has "exergaming" or "exertainment." Exergaming, also called "fitness gaming," is a new marketing term coined to describe the combination of exercise equipment or aerobic workout regimens with video games. These products seek to make physical exercise more attractive to people by adding the mentally engaging elements of video games to the activity.

Konami's *Dance Dance Revolution (DDR)*, originally released in Japan in 1991 as an arcade game, is an example of a video game that mixes physical activity with game play mechanics. *DDR* uses the special input controller (see Figure 8.1): a dance pad, with four panels, up, down, left, and right, arranged around where the player stands. The player presses the panels with his or her feet in response to arrows that flash on the game's screen. The arrows are synchronized to the rhythm or beat of a song played by the game, and success depends on the player's ability to time his or her steps accordingly. Since its days in the arcade, *DDR* has been released as specialized cabinets that players can buy to play at home and for game consoles like the Sony PlayStation.

FIGURE 8.1

Dance Dance Revolution input controller

© Imelda Kataraharajan. Used with Permission

RedOctane, makers of Ignition Pad, the top-selling dance pad in 2004, created the Get Up & Move PR campaign in January 2004. According to the Get Up & Move Web site, Tanya Jessen, the campaign spokesperson, lost 95 pounds (43 kilograms) by repeatedly playing the *Dance Dance Revolution* series of games. Dean Ku, speaking at the Serious Games Summit at the 2005 Game Developer's conference, said that the campaign grew out of RedOctane's decision to stay close to the dance game community. After receiving a lot of e-mails from players who were losing weight, the company decided to see if it could help promote this type of wellness program. Tanya Jessen, for example, didn't start dancing to lose weight. It happened naturally as she began playing the game and noticed a slimmer figure. In addition to helping players lose weight, the Get Up & Move campaign had a huge sales impact for *DDR* and its sequel, *DDR2*.

DDR has been the subject of a number of studies in recent years. In a 2005 research study, George Graham and Stephen Yang of Penn State University measured the heart rates of children who played *DDR* for 45 minutes. The researchers found that the children had an average heart rate of 144 beats per minute when playing, compared to the average resting heart rate of 60 to 70 beats per minute. The increased heart rate increases the metabolism and causes the body to burn more calories.

In another study currently underway, researchers at West Virginia University also aim to study children playing *DDR*. The six-month study, coordinated with the state's Public Employees Insurance Agency, examines the possibility of cutting claim costs from obesity. In the same vein, Bryan Haddock, an Associate Professor of Kinesiology at Cal State San Bernardino, is planning a summer 2005 study with Riverside-based game company, QMotions, on how exergaming products can help reduce childhood obesity.

In 2003, Sony released the EyeToy (see Figure 8.2), a digital camera device for the PlayStation 2 that allows players to interact with specially designed games by moving their bodies, including their head, arms, hands, and legs. Lisa Liddane, in her February 26, 2005, article for the *Orange County Register*, "Acting Out: Kids Get into the Game," described a nine year old boy playing *EyeToy: Play*, a collection of mini-games: "As the animated fighters jump from balconies on the screen, Mitchell jabs swiftly into the air to knock them down. He executes a sharp kick with his left leg and bounces an opponent out of the screen. Every now and then, he shuffles left and right like a boxer. For bonus points, he breaks wooden boards left and right."

Following the examples of *DDR* and the EyeToy, there is an emerging market for new controllers and interfaces, and accompanying games, that allow players to get involved with video games in new, highly active ways. The Cateye *GameBike* and the Reebok *CyberRider* hook up to a game console, such as the PlayStation 2 or XBox, so that the player can pedal a stationary bike and play games that involve driving or riding vehicles. Priced at $1200 (as of this writing), these peripherals show the revenue potential for exergaming.

FIGURE 8.2

EyeToy

© Imelda Kartarahardja.
Used with Permission

At the 2005 Electronic Entertainment Expo (E3), QMotions showed off its baseball controller for console and PC video games, adding to its line of full-motion video game controllers. Many other companies were also showcasing their new exercise-oriented gaming products. Such controllers make the experience of playing the video game versions of sports like baseball and golf much more like the original sport. At the least, with these controllers the player's interaction with the game exceeds the standard "activity" of clicking buttons and pushing a mouse around.

Mark Wolf, in his book *The Medium of the Video Game*, listed other games that involved physical activity that have been released over the years. Many of these were full-sized arcade games, and players would sit inside or ride on top of the consoles. The player's physical movements control the game to simulate everything from driving to flying, pedaling a bicycle (*Prop Cycle*, 1993), or holding ski pole handles while standing on moveable skis (*Alpine Racer*, 1995). Other examples include Sega's *Top Skater* (1997), which has a skateboard, and Namco's *Final Furlong* (1997), a game about racehorse riding.

Another use of serious games is in sex education and/or the prevention of sexually transmitted diseases, such as herpes and HIV/AIDS. The very serious nature of the subject matter, combined with the political and religious controversies, could be enough to make designers look for less-troublesome arenas, but these types of games are just another type of self-management. An example of a game that does tackle these issues is Will Interactive's *HIV Interactive Nights Out*. Designed to promote HIV prevention, the game was given to over 200 soldiers ages 19 to 29 years old in a study by the U.S. Army. The study found that more than half of the soldiers voluntarily played the game more than once and that the program reinforced the participants' existing inclinations to protect themselves against HIV infection.

Exergaming Case Study—responDESIGN's *Yourself!Fitness*

In late 2004 and early 2005, responDESIGN, a Portland, Oregon, company devoted to creating "games that are good for you," released *Yourself!Fitness* for the XBox, PC, and PlayStation 2. Designed to surpass fitness videos and self-help books, *Yourself!Fitness* bills itself as "the first game title created solely to improve the health and fitness of the user." With information provided by the player, the game creates a personalized fitness program, and Maya, a virtual personal trainer, coaches the player through the training sessions.

Yourself!Fitness incorporates yoga, Pilates, cardio fitness, strength training, flexibility exercises, and targeted weight loss routines. *Yourself!Fitness* will also integrate any training equipment the player has. Unlike home fitness DVDs, which only provide a list of options that users can choose from and a static set of exercises and activities, company co-founder Phineas Barnes said the game provides all the tools to create a "personal, interactive, goal-oriented fitness program at home." The personalization is derived from information inputted by the user about his or her personal fitness level at the start of *Yourself!Fitness*. *Yourself!Fitness* then creates a customized fitness program based on user fitness and preferences. Add to that full user control over the camera angles, the playback speed of the exercise demonstration, different environments, and adjustable order of exercises each day, and the product offers a lot of advantages over the traditional home fitness DVD.

Barnes does not consider *Yourself!Fitness* a game. Though *Yourself!Fitness* employs game elements like a system of rewards, including new environments, new music, and new levels, its primary aim is to be a personal fitness program. Even so, it was important to responDESIGN to make the product fun and engaging.

Yourself!Fitness required a development budget of less than $500,000, which, Barnes pointed out, is a fraction of the budgets required for most console titles, and it was created with 100 percent game technology. The 21 members of the project team, which included a number of fitness experts, put special effort into guaranteeing correct joint movement in Maya, the virtual personal trainer. As seen in Figure 8.3, this ensures that when Maya demonstrates a particular exercise or technique, the player is seeing it done exactly right.

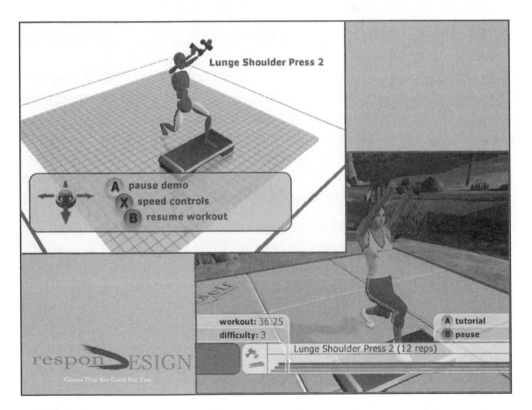

FIGURE 8.3

Yourself!Fitness

© responDESIGN. Used with Permission

The home fitness market sells 30 to 40 million fitness videos and DVDs each year, with 90 percent of those purchases being made by women. That is the market segment reponDESIGN wanted to tap into with *Yourself!Fitness*, and so, the game was designed to appeal to women. However, the company has heard from men who have started using *Yourself!Fitness* as well. Getting men to participate, Barnes noted, is considered a significant achievement in the home fitness market.

Unlike video game sales, home fitness sales do not peak at Christmas and are at the highest just after the beginning of the year, in January and February. responDESIGN has targeted this period for its marketing. However, with its game-like properties, *Yourself!Fitness* can capitalize on both the shortage of new video games on store shelves just before Christmas and the general home fitness craze that follows the holiday season.

This combination of elements from two markets, though, has also forced responDESIGN to explore alternatives to the normal video game retail outlets. Further, because the product resembles a home fitness DVD, but isn't a DVD, and requires either a computer or game console, the company has also run into issues selling to some home fitness retail outlets. Despite those issues, responDESIGN has been able to reach mothers in video game stores, professional women at stores like Best Buy, and a wide range of female buyers at Nordstrom. It continues to look for new marketing venues and would like to be able to reach even into the hardcore game player arena.

Barnes said that responDESIGN has big plans for the future. Eventually, the company expects *Yourself!Fitness* to be a full "health lifestyle monitoring tool." responDESIGN wants users to be able to track their progress through the use of networked equipment and next-generation game consoles. This tracking could even extend throughout the day, covering diet and other lifestyle aspects. "The more information you plug in," Barnes added, "the more access to health and fitness resources you'll have through the program."

Training and Simulation

In January 2004, J.C. Rosser, Jr., P.J. Lynch, L.A. Haskamp, A. Yalif, D.A. Gentile, and L. Giammaria presented a paper at the Medicine Meets Virtual Reality Conference, in Newport Beach, California.

Entitled "Are Video Game Players Better at Laparoscopic Surgery?", the paper outlined their results of a study initiated to prove or disprove these hypotheses: "Surgeons with past video game experience will perform better in a standardized laparoscopic skill and suturing program," and "video games are correlated with better performance in a standardized laparoscopic skill and suturing program."

The study lasted from May through August of 2003 and included 33 surgeons, comprised of 21 residents and 12 attending physicians, at Beth Israel Medical Center in New York City. The study emphasized dexterity with the doctor's non-dominant hand, two-handed choreography, targeting, and 2D depth perception skills. The games chosen for the study were based on "perceived correlation with laparoscopic skills and suturing." Overall, surgeons who had played video games for three or more hours per week had 37 precent fewer errors than those who never played video games and were 27 percent faster at laparoscopic drills and suturing tasks.

The same study proposed the following advantages of using video games in surgical training:

- Cost-effective platform for training and skill development
- Wide availability and portability of video games
- Future physician recruitment of video game generation
- Implications for the prevention and reduction of errors

The authors of the study even talked about the possible benefits of using video games as warm-up exercises before certain surgical procedures and looked forward to the creation of surgery-specific video games.

There are many more health professionals than just surgeons. There are general practitioners, specialists, nurses, physical therapists, emergency medical technicians, professional caregivers, and more, and they can all benefit from similar training games. The Rosser *et al* study, plus other studies, has shown that practicing a task virtually with video game-like simulators has a beneficial effect, improving performance at a rate similar to actually performing the task.

There have been a few games created over the years with that goal in mind. In *Auscultation*, created by medical publisher C.V. Mosby, the player has a headset and listens to heart murmurs, placing the stethoscope on different areas of a man's chest. Auscultation is the medical term for listening to sounds in body organs for diagnosis and treatment. An electronic stethoscope is one of the game controllers.

In the 1970s, Judy Tyrer assisted in the creation of patient management simulations for training doctors. The simulations, paid for by drug companies, were close to "advergaming" in that they touted the benefits of new drugs in handling certain medical situations, but the simulations did try to accurately portray those situations, offering a decision tree of possible action choices and showing the results of the actions chosen. For example, if it were an ulcer patient, the doctor would go through the simulation, choosing treatments and lab work. Afterward came the sales pitch: "This is what you did, and this is the traditional method of treating that condition, and, look, we have this great new drug, and this is how the drug works."

More recently, BreakAway Games received a federal grant to create *Pulse!*, a virtual learning space for healthcare professionals. Replete with virtual patients powered by AI, *Pulse!* would be the first immersive interactive environment where civilian and military medical personnel could practice clinical procedures and even prepare for bioterrorist events. At the time of this writing, BreakAway Games was also working on *Code Orange*, a simulation that would help prepare doctors to deal with mass casualties.

Similarly, the 2004 Games For Health conference showcased certain games like *ACLS Interactive*. *ACLS Interactive* by Mosby is an advanced cardiac life support (ACLS) simulator that lets emergency medical technicians (EMTs) and paramedics practice cardiac life-saving skills. The simulation includes a variety of scenarios, including the emergency room and the critical care unit.

Pamela Andreatta, M.D., Director of the Clinical Simulation Center at the University of Michigan Medical School in Ann Arbor, talked about two types of surgical simulation in John McIntosh's article, "Sci-Fi Medicine," for the Summer 2005 issue of *Remedy*. The first focuses on software-driven models of adults and children. These models, which are physiologically and anatomically functional and correct, can be programmed to create any series of physical events or medical conditions. Once the cases are set up, physicians, nurses, and EMTs can be run through the situation, managing the scenario as practice before they have to face it in the real world.

The second type of surgical simulation is even more virtual. The Clinical Simulation Center has a facility they call "the Cave," which is described as "a virtual reality holodeck straight from Star Trek." The Cave is a room with four walls that project three-dimensional images. The trainee, wearing 3D glasses, stands in the room and is immersed in a virtual reality. In this environment, the physician can practice a procedure over and over so that, as Dr. Andreatta said, "the psychomotor aspects of the procedure become automatic." The Cave provides a quiet, calm atmosphere to help the surgeon gain confidence in his or her abilities, and, Dr. Andreatta added, "It's an obvious boon for patient safety."

Mental Health—Game Therapy

Games also have proven useful in mental health. Studies have shown that people respond to games in many of the same ways that they respond to real-life events. They react with fear in frightening situations, excitement during high-speed races, and so on. Thus in a sense, games are real experiences, and learning how to face a situation in a game can provide the foundation for learning how to face the situation in real life.

Diagnosis

Doctors may soon be using video games to diagnose some disorders, such as attention deficit and hyperactive disorder (ADHD) and post-traumatic stress disorder (PTSD). The batch of signals sent to the computer by a player's hand on the joystick forms patterns. One of these patterns has been isolated by Skip Rizzo, a psychological-cyberneticist at ICT, as an identifier for children with ADHD. Rizzo is also using *Full Spectrum Warrior*, a game developed by ICT, to diagnose and treat PTSD in Iraq war veterans.

Additional psychological, cognitive, and neurological disorders that mental health professionals hope to be able to diagnose and treat with games are Rett

Syndrome, schizophrenia, various phobias, learning impairments, language impairments, and more.

Facing Fears

An area of mental health that has seen some success by modifying (creating "mods") of commercial, off-the-shelf games is in the treatment of phobias. Images and models of the feared object or creature (such as spiders, snakes, or cotton balls) can be added to the game and presented to the player-patient in a realistic situation.

Sometimes the games used do not have to be modified. Agoraphobia (a fear of open spaces) and phobias related to driving cars have seen some success with driving games, like *Midtown Madness* published by Microsoft, that feature realistic urban settings.

Psychologists want to move past these simple examples and tackle more complex disorders, like PTSD. A key aspect of treating PTSD is having the patient confront the event under the supervision of a trained professional. A study following the treatment of PTSD in Vietnam veterans found limited success using simulations. However, the results are not conclusive because the studies occurred twenty years after the return of the Vietnam veterans. Currently, a study is underway in Iraq hoping to help the soldiers there.

Similar to PTSD treatment is stress hardening. Stress hardening is conditioning the patient prior to a potentially stressful event. In both cases, the games require realistic rendering of environments and situations, including situations involving people.

Video games are being used for therapeutic interventions and exposure therapy. In Europe, simulations have been used to treat eating disorders like anorexia.

Socializing and Social Skills

Social games, whether video games or more traditional games like board games and card games, have been seen to help the elderly stay healthy and mentally alert. Other benefits for the elderly have included improvements in reaction time, well-being, cognitive functioning, memory functioning, emotional status, and so on.

Second Life, the 3D digital world created by Linden Lab, has been used for a variety of mental health issues. The realism modeled in the game, and the ability to create private worlds, has proven ideal for some types of treatment. In one case, abused children in Portuguese safe houses are being taught social skills, team building, computer skills, and so on within the game. Also in *Second Life*, but in separate in-world "islands," adults suffering from conditions such as cerebral palsy, autism, and Asperger's syndrome are given a chance to have normal social and personal interaction in a judgment-free environment.

Self-Discovery

Whether intentionally or accidentally, the choices available in a game imply a system of morality, of right and wrong. "Right" choices are rewarded by the game, while "wrong" choices are penalized. How players respond to choices presented within a game can prove valuable to mental professionals and to the players themselves.

The Journey to Wild Divine, described as the "first 'inner-active' computer adventure," uses biofeedback equipment: Sensors on three of the player's fingers track heart rate variability and skin conductance. Variations in these measurements control the player's progress through the game. As the player completes the 40 "energy events," the game is teaching the person how to better control physical, mental, and emotional states.

Such biofeedback technology, combined with techniques developed to keep NASA astronauts and U.S. Air Force pilots attentive in the cockpit, may help treat ADHD. Players of the Play Attention Learning System by Unique Logic and Technology use biofeedback and visual tracking technology built into a special helmet to control a video game. As they learn to control the game, they improve their powers of focus and their attention span.

Treating Phobias Case Study— the Virtual Reality Medical Center

Therapists at the Virtual Reality Medical Center (VRMC) use virtual reality exposure therapy (3D computer simulation) in combination with physiological monitoring and feedback to treat panic and anxiety disorders.

According to the VRMC Web site, the conditions treated include specific phobias, such as fear of flying, fear of driving, fear of heights, fear of public speaking, fear of thunderstorms, claustrophobia, agoraphobia, social phobia, panic disorder, and PTSD as a result of severe motor vehicle accidents.

Dr. Mark Wiederhold, President of VRMC, said that about 5000 therapy sessions have utilized simulations with a success rate of over 92 percent. Thus simulations have proven to be an excellent addition to behavior therapy.

Dr. Wiederhold repeatedly stressed the importance of the therapist in the treatment. Simulations are just one of the tools used throughout the process. Just as serious games will not replace a talented teacher in the classroom, neither will they replace the role of the therapist in treating psychological disorders. Beyond helping the patient into and through the simulation, the therapist also talks to the patient offline, outside the VR, to teach coping and relaxation techniques such as meditation and deep breathing.

The therapists at VRMC use simulations to expose the patient to the fear stimulus, but in a gradual way. The patient is not fully immersed in the simulation immediately. For example, if the patient has a fear of heights, the first visit might consist of the patient being shown an elevator and nothing more. Over the sequence of the treatment, though, the patient is brought deeper and deeper into the scenario. In a typical one-hour session, the simulation might be used for 20 to 30 minutes.

The simulations can be anywhere on the spectrum of reality and imagination, Dr. Wiederhold said. High fidelity, a strict adherence to reality, is not necessary. The graphics and the action can be cartoonish, if that seems a better fit for the particular therapy.

Over the years, VRMC has used a lot of different kinds of game engines to create their simulations. The simulations aren't really games, but they do have certain aspects that are similar to games. For instance, in a driving simulation, the patient would have to get into a car, drive the car, and successfully navigate the roads. Thus, the patient has been given a task, like in a game, to go from Point A to Point B. Despite that, there isn't any kind of scoring and usually no time limits are imposed.

Assessing the success of the therapy doesn't require any complex in-simulation tracking. Usually, Dr. Wiederhold said, the assessment is that if the patient was afraid of heights before, and now isn't afraid and can go up an elevator in real life, then it worked. If the patient had a fear of public speaking, then a presentation in front of people is proof of a cure. For a person afraid of flying, success is getting on a plane and going someplace. That isn't to say that the simulation can't provide tracked assessment, just that it's not always necessary in the case of therapy.

Assessing whether or not the patient has been successfully treated for more complex disorders, like PTSD, is more complicated. The number of factors involved in such disorders precludes a simple test. There would need to be specific measures, designed according to clinical protocols. Also, reducing the symptoms is only one of the goals of treating PTSD.

DEVELOPING GAMES FOR HEALTHCARE

Designing and developing games for healthcare has many of the same issues and requirements as creating serious games for the military and other government agencies (discussed in Chapters 4 and 5), as well as those for education and nonprofit organizations (discussed in Chapter 6).

Design Issues

Serious games for healing and recovery cannot be expected to replace doctors or therapists. For this reason, the games need to incorporate many of the same features required in other areas, like military training and education, that empower the experts and help them do their jobs better. These features include:

- Observer modes for the therapist or overseeing physician
- Coaching options (from observer mode)
- Pause/Play options to quickly suspend/resume the game
- Easy creation of patient-specific missions/levels with variable levels of immersion/intensity
- Age-appropriateness, based on patient age or therapist recommendation

In addition, flexibility with game controllers and displays will be useful in many cases, which would allow the game to be accessible to as many patients as possible. When designing a game for pain management, for example, the most important specification could be that the game be playable with one hand controller because usually the other hand has an IV attached. Also, the game might need to support a head-mounted VR viewer.

Like serious games for the military, serious games for healthcare are more likely to be simulations, with a need to accurately portray reality. Whether it's showing the organs in an open chest cavity for physicians to practice invasive surgery, or re-creating a stressful situation from a patient's past so that they can face it again as part of their treatment, these type of serious games will place a premium on accuracy. As Dr. Wiederhold mentioned, though, serious games created for mental or psychological therapy have more latitude in this regard. In cases like pain distraction, the content of the game need not be related to healthcare in any way.

Finally, when designing a game to be used in healthcare, the resulting game should not exacerbate the problem it's supposed to solve nor add new problems. For example, a game intended for physical therapy should not force the player to make small, repetitive movements and thereby cause a repetitive stress injury.

In the same way, serious games created to help mental patients or to deal with psychological disorders should be sensitive to the needs of patients and their treatment and should allow the therapist full control over the intensity of the situation presented in the simulation. For example, a public speaking simulation should be adjustable for the size and attentiveness of the audience, a ride on a virtual airplane flight should be adjustably smooth or turbulent, and so forth.

These design considerations make it imperative that game developers find experts in the particular healthcare area that the game is intended for. Physicians, surgeons, nurses, physical therapists, psychologists, researchers, and other healthcare professionals have all endured long, intensive training and it would be the height of presumption, and probably disastrous, for a game developer to think that the input from those professionals isn't crucial.

Beyond providing accuracy, the professionals associated with a serious game for healthcare lend credibility to the project and may prove valuable when looking for funding for the project. The participation of professionals could also be crucial if the game requires certification from an overseeing body like a medical school curriculum board or the American Medical Association.

Pitching

The markets for serious games for healthcare include a wide selection. There are hospitals, clinics, private practice physicians and specialists, therapists, personal trainers, and even consumers. There are also corporations, non-profit organizations (NPOs) and non-government organizations (NGOs) who may be interested in educating, training, or informing any of the listed groups. Despite this wide selection, it may not be obvious where to begin looking for funding or customers.

One of the first issues that must be considered when pitching serious games to medical and mental health hospitals and organizations is the cost. As Dr. Wiederhold was quoted earlier in this chapter as saying, "If it's not inexpensive, it won't be used." On the other hand, the cost of healthcare is a highly political issue in the United States and around the world and presenting serious games as a possible way to decrease the costs of treatment or speed recovery will almost certainly get attention.

Like the educators discussed in Chapter 6, though, healthcare professionals are already overworked and presented with a plethora of possible treatment options. Unless the developer can show a definitive benefit to using a serious game for treatment, either in reduced cost to treat the condition or improvements in healing or recovery rate, they aren't likely to be interested.

When asked about getting grants and/or other funding to develop serious games for health care, Dr. Wiederhold pointed out that there are announcements and long-established dates for the contract bidding process. The National Institutes of Health (NIH) grants, for example, are given out four times a year and there are other government contracts available.

Some corporations, especially biotech startups and pharmaceutical companies, are interested in serious games for healthcare, as are a number of non-profit organizations. He did not recommend seeking funding at hospitals. The market is not huge, he added, but it will grow if the costs remain low.

In the U.S., NIH and the National Institute of Mental Health (NIMH) both participate in the Small Business Innovative Research (SBIR) program described in Chapter 4. The same participation requirements, funding ranges, and development phases described in that chapter apply to these organizations as well. SBIR's for NIH and NIMH will focus on biological and mental health issues, including diagnosis, treatment, and prevention.

For many NPOs and NGOs, games are a key attraction of their Web pages. These games, however, tend to be very small and very simple. The effectiveness of these games, often created by game enthusiasts within the organization, varies widely and as this type of Web-site game has proliferated around the Web, their appeal has waned. Thus, there is a need for the deeper game play and greater engagement that professional game developers can provide. Game developers with experience in the retail arena have the skills and tools to raise these games to a whole new level. By utilizing their experience to create compelling games that drive home the theme or message of the organization, they can help those organizations increase their appeal and broaden their reach.

To be attractive to such organizations, developers will need to keep their costs down. NPOs and NGOs often have very tight budgets, relying on grants from the government, private parties, or even other NPOs. The money available for games can range from nothing to tens of thousands or even, in some cases, hundreds of thousands of dollars. Not large, but still possibly substantial. The Starlight Starbright Children's Foundation is an example of a NPO that has funded game development through grants.

As we mentioned in Chapter 6, "Educational Games," partnerships and sponsorships can be helpful to the developer looking for funding. The Robert Woods Foundation, for example, an organization that "seeks to improve the health and health care of all Americans," does not accept applications from individuals. The foundation's grants require the sponsorship of another NPO. So even if a NPO or NGO does not directly provide funding, by being partnered with one, the developer may find more doors opening up and more opportunities.

Development Issues

Just as there are many possible markets for healthcare games, there a wide variety of types of serious game for healthcare and an equally wide variety of ways to approach their development. Sometimes, as in a number of the simulations described by Dr. Wiederhold, the requirements can be met by modifying or "modding" an existing game. Other times, a fully immersive simulation will be built from pre-existing video game technology or even from scratch. Pre-existing technology, of course, is usually the most cost-effective approach, which is important.

Serious games for healthcare do not present too many new issues. As was mentioned earlier, they face some of the same issues as developing serious games for the military, government agencies, education, and even corporations. For example, the budgets can be much like those in education (that is, hard to find) or ranging up to several hundred thousand dollars like those for corporate training games.

Also, like the government games discussed in Chapter 5, many of these games will be highly specialized, created for a single, specific purpose. An entire game world need not be created if the only thing required for the game to be useful is a single building with an elevator and an up button.

Accessibility and Specialized Controllers

Accessibility was discussed in earlier chapters in relation to government-mandated availability of training tools to people with disabilities. In healthcare, though, accessibility takes a different form. Many of the people playing serious games for health care will be at least temporarily disabled or impaired. The ability to hold a controller in two hands, or even one hand, cannot be assumed. This is why there has been a strong emphasis on VR interfaces like headsets and gauntlets. However, the use of the eyes, ears, or voice cannot be assumed in all cases.

Games integrated with specialized controllers, like stationary bikes or dance pads, can be as realistic or fantastic as the designer thinks is useful. In these games, engagement of the player is possibly the most important aspect, after ensuring that the exercise is well balanced. Specialized controllers also offer game developers the possibility of new revenue streams, from the sale of the needed hardware along with the game itself.

Sensitive Information and Patient Privacy

A patient's personal information and medical conditions are considered extremely private and they are the subject of laws and regulations in most countries. If a serious game uses or collects any information from the patient, steps must be taken to comply with any applicable privacy laws. The data must be protected from casual observation or unauthorized retrieval, and it must be encrypted if it's to be sent out over the Internet.

This will not affect all serious games for healthcare. For instance, the games used at VRMC never utilize patient information. They also do not go home with the patients, so maintaining privacy is less of an issue.

CONCLUSION

Video games have already made an impression on healthcare, from helping surgeons improve their skills to distracting children during painful medical procedures to helping the mentally ill overcome their phobias, and even motivating sedentary "couch potatoes" to get up and move. As video games and virtual reality technology improve, the possibilities for serious games in health care will grow.

In healthcare, as in the military, lives are often on the line. And not just physical lives. Both the mental and emotional lives of the players can also be affected. This makes these serious games even more serious. However, game developers who are willing to work alongside healthcare professionals have the chance to create a powerful, positive impact.

In the next chapter, we will explore the smaller, more personal serious game markets of political games, religious games, and art games.

Political, Religious, and Art Games

Most of the serious games and serious game markets that we have covered in this book have focused on knowledge transfer (traditional teaching) and skill transfer (training). In this chapter, we will cover the third aspect of education: attitude transfer (informing). Specifically, we will look at serious games created with or for a political, religious, and/or artistic agenda.

The content of video games and the interaction with that content has often come under scrutiny. The abstract images of early games like *Pong* and *Pac-Man* generated little comment. The graphics capability of computers and video games has improved since then and now realistic images can be presented. Some game designers have insisted that the images represented in games have no relation to their real world counterparts. The gameplay mechanics, they say, reduce the images to simple tokens that provide specific bonuses or modifiers within the game. The general public, especially religious and political leaders, tend to disagree, and so do an increasing number of game designers.

In their article, "Games Get Serious 2.0," Henry Jenkins and Kurt Squire wrote that changing the artwork of a popular game such as *Grand Theft Auto* changes the meaning of the game. Replacing the images of cars, guns, and gangsters with tricycles, flowers, and little girls would, even if the rest of the gameplay remained unchanged, create an entirely different meaning to the game. This is because players come from a culture where certain objects have certain meanings, and meaning is important in education and in art.

The representational nature of game content, its relation to the culture or cultures it comes from, and its ability to transmit statements about the content is the topic of this chapter. Just like movies, books, or any other type of art, video games present a view of the world. This is true whether or not the game designer intended to present such a world view. But what if the designer intentionally and explicitly espoused a view?

We have split this chapter into three sections so that we can focus on each area in turn. However, there can be a lot of overlap between politics, religion, and art. Sometimes this overlap is intentional and sometimes it's not. Intentional or unintentional, it is often inevitable. Throughout history, both religion and art have come out in support of or in opposition to political figures and governments. Political powers have attempted to regulate both religion and art. Furthermore, religion and art have had a tumultuous relationship of their own, separate from secular politics.

POLITICAL GAMES

Ian Bogost, an Assistant Professor at the Georgia Institute of Technology, moderated the panel, "Games as Mass Media Dialogue Devices," at the 2004 Serious Games Summit in Washington, D.C. Bogost described games as a socially expressive media with as much power as any other medium and capable of expression across the spectrum of the human experience. Bogost, who is also a founding partner of the company Persuasive Games in Atlanta, Georgia, defined political games as "rhetorical tools that teach, persuade, and influence through simulated experiences." In other words, they are "video games with an agenda."

Video games, like TV, film, books, and music, are a medium with a long and deep cultural reach, both reflecting and affecting the cultures that create them. Just as *America's Army* has been seen by some as an electronic ambassador of goodwill, anti-U.S. games exist and are being created with a very different message, making video games the latest tool in (dis)information warfare and propaganda.

Political games are those games that promote or come out against specific government policy positions or aspects of government. Policy positions include laws, regulations, ordinances, environmentalism, race relations, international relations, equal rights, religion, free speech, national borders, military spending, public works projects, and on and on. Aspects of government are such things as the electoral process, campaigning and voting, legislative procedures, the party system, the court system, military service, and so on.

Often, political games have an obvious bias for or against whatever issue, position, or personality the game is about. This isn't always the case, of course. Sometimes, the game is an honest attempt to explore both sides of a contentious issue.

Survey of Political Games

Chris Crawford's game *Energy Czar*, a simulation of the energy crisis, released in 1980 for Atari, might be considered one of the earliest political games. In 1985, his *Balance of Power*, a Cold War simulation, continued his trend of mixing current world events, computer games, and his own views of how the world worked. That these games are considered classics of the video game era shows how effectively they merged entertainment and editorial.

The 2004 presidential election in the United States generated a number of political games, some little more than animated political cartoons, but others with interesting depth and features. Persuasive Games created the *Howard Dean for Iowa* game for the Howard Dean campaign to educate Dean supporters in the mechanics of grass roots outreach programs. The purpose of the game was to encourage supporters to engage in campaign activities, such as canvassing for votes or displaying signs (see Figure 9.1). Each player

FIGURE 9.1

The *Howard Dean for Iowa* game

© Persuasive Games. Used with Permission

in the game affected the results of other players and could communicate with each other through instant messaging (IM) capabilities. Thus the game helped promote a stronger sense of community among Dean supporters.

State elections can be just as contentious as national ones. Persuasive Games also designed the *Take Back Illinois* game, which was initially sponsored by the Citizens to elect Tom Cross for the 2004 election. The game educated Illinois voters on Republican viewpoints for four key campaign issues. As can be seen from Figure 9.2, the player has the "God view" vantage used in many simulation games.

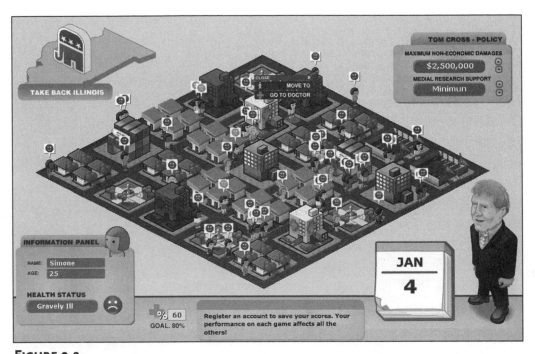

FIGURE 9.2

The *Take Back Illinois* game

© Persuasive Games. Used with Permission

Beyond electioneering, political games can be used to effectively present a viewpoint about divisive issues or current events. They are like interactive versions of a newspaper's Op-Ed pages. More importantly, the viewpoint is dramatized through graphics and design choices. The terrorist attack on the World Trade Center in New York City in 2001 has been the basis for a number of serious games. *September 12th*, a game by Newsgaming.com, insists that it "is not a game" and gives players the option to fire cruise missiles at terrorists in a densely populated Middle Eastern city. "You can shoot. Or not." The game doesn't end. It can't end. As the cruise missiles strike their targets, civilians first weep over the casualties, and then morph into terrorists.

The ongoing conflict between Israelis and Palestinians has been a flash-point for different groups. *Under Ash* and its follow-up, *Under Siege*, takes the Palestinian viewpoint and is sometimes considered a response to the way

Arabs are portrayed in *America's Army*. The success of *America's Army* and its ample promotion, as shown in Figure 9.3, has not endeared it to everyone. Many consider the game pure propaganda, promoting U.S. interests and providing only a narrow view of how the U.S. conducts military operations overseas. To counteract this perceived propaganda, some independent developers outside the United States, who do not see the U.S. and U.S. intervention in a positive light, have begun creating games with the U.S. as the villains.

FIGURE 9.3

America's Army at E3: Goodwill ambassador or American propaganda?

© Sande Chen. Used with Permission

A group of graduate students at Carnegie Mellon University has taken a more even-handed approach to the Middle East conflict. In *PeaceMaker*, a single-player game, the player takes the role of either the Israeli Prime Minister or the Palestinian President. The player is faced with a variety of events, from diplomatic negotiations to suicide bombers, and must interact with eight other political leaders and social groups. The goal of the game is to come up with a peaceful and stable resolution to the conflict before the player's term of office is up. *PeaceMaker* strives to present both sides of the conflict in a balanced way, without saying that either side is right or wrong. The designers want the game to be an educational tool for informing teenagers on both sides of the issue and help bring about peace in the region.

Likewise, Breakaway Games' *A Force More Powerful* seeks peaceful solutions and promotes non-violent protest. Designed in partnership with the International Center on Nonviolent Conflict and York Zimmerman, Inc., *A Force More Powerful* is a turn-based strategy game designed to instruct activists engaged in non-violent challenges to dictatorships and government policies.

Other countries similarly face heated national debates. Julian Oliver, the director of SelectParks, a media lab in Melbourne, Australia, along with two other artists, created *Escape From Woomera*, a virtual reconstruction of four Australian immigration-detention centers. In the game, the player is seeking to escape the detention center and immigrate illegally to Australia. *Escape From Woomera*'s purpose was to raise awareness of the refugee detention centers in Australia, a hot political topic in the country, and according to the game's Web site, to create a game that didn't "create heroes out of professional killers and U.S. marines."

Political Game Case Study—*PeaceMaker*

According to producer/artist Asaf Burak, an Israeli graduate student at the Entertainment Technology Center (ETC) at Carnegie Mellon University in Pittsburgh, Pennsylvania, *PeaceMaker* (see Figure 9.4) is intended to be the first "peace game." *PeaceMaker* is, he admitted, "a political game, a simulation of the Israeli-Palestinian conflict," but it also strives to be an educational game. "While [the game] deals with burning political issues," Burak said, "its main aim is to teach and educate. We would like to teach Israeli and Palestinian teenagers how both sides can work together to achieve a lasting peace and coexistence."

FIGURE 9.4

PeaceMaker

© Asaf Burak, Tim Sweeney, Eric Keylor, and Ross Popoff. Used with Permission.

Tim Sweeney, lead designer for *PeaceMaker*, also stressed the educational aspects of the game. "Playing [*PeaceMaker*]," he said, "can both ground you with knowledge of the conflict" and provide a deeper lesson of how a peaceful balance could be achieved. "Our game is not unusual that it has a theme, but our conscious decision to use [a theme] and set it towards peace is different from the norm."

Burak, a native of Israel, wanted to explore video games as an interactive medium and art form. He considered video games as one of the most powerful communication mediums of the modern era, but he was unhappy with the current offerings. Modern games, he said, "barely begin to exploit the possibilities of addressing the full range of human emotions and needs. I wanted to design new game models, which are much broader in their moral message and opportunities for expression and which focus on construction rather than destruction. I thought we should aim at game models which are attractive to both genders and which will provide true revelations to their participants." He added, "Most video games deal with conquest, war, and destruction." With *PeaceMaker*, he wanted to create "a game for the future—a game which will teach the player that peace and cohabitation, not war and annihilation, [are] the only real strategy worth fighting for."

With that goal, and with his background as an Israeli, Burak pitched the idea for *PeaceMaker* to the university faculty. Though the ETC didn't provide funding, the faculty did give their approval for the project and provided access to computers and advisors. The ETC encouraged the team, which also included programmer Eric Keylor and writer/designer Ross Popoff, to spend time building the game itself, instead of just a demo. "They wanted us to go all the way and prove our concept with a playable version," Burak said.

PeaceMaker attempts to be fun, but, said Sweeney, "fun comes from many places." The goal with *PeaceMaker*, he went on, "is better defined as engaging the player rather than helping them have fun." The first step is getting the players to "accept the game and not believe it to be unrealistic, juvenile, biased, or boring. Once they're receptive to that, they can pick up our message simply by playing along. The lesson of the game is deeply integrated with the gameplay. Decisions made that are aggressive and one-sided lead to losing, while winning requires balanced and careful action."

Burak agreed. The message was "the most important thing for us," he said. However, to convey the message, he saw the need for the game to be an attractive, challenging, and compelling experience. Without that, he didn't see how the game could achieve their goals. He compared *PeaceMaker* to documentary TV shows and films. "Most [documentaries], especially when dealing with conflicts and wars, are hard to watch, but provide a different kind of experience which is quite powerful."

The team faced a wide range of issues while designing the game. The first problem, Sweeney said, came from the complexity of the game and its subject matter. Restricting the game to a "strategy simulation" offered them a project "which could be achievable in our time frame and budget." After that came the research, culling details from news reports, and expert opinions to get to what they called the core issues of the conflict, and then figuring out how to simulate those issues as a system within the game.

To keep the game from being a boring history lesson, the player needed to be able to start taking actions quickly. To that end, the player's in-game actions are broad strokes, Sweeney said, instead of a detailed tactical simulation. "The flavor of the complex realities involved still comes across," he added, "through the feel of the game, even though the mechanics are not complex."

Another challenge was creating convincing artificial intelligence for the various NPCs in the game. "We have to simulate the reactions of different [political and social groups]," Keylor said. To add to the challenge, these were political and social groups that existed in the real world. Their behavior had to be reasonable and not stereotypical responses that could be declared caricatures or biased.

Burak, due to his closeness to the situation being modeled, faced a different challenge. "For me, as an Israeli," he said, "the biggest challenge was to design an unbiased game." To better guarantee a balanced view for the project, the team involved Palestinians in the project from the beginning. Two Palestinian students from Pittsburgh, Rana El-Hindi and Hanadie Yousef, volunteered to help with the project and provided comments and feedback about images and wording included in the game.

Though *PeaceMaker* was originally targeted at Israeli and Palestinian teenagers, the ones closest to the conflict and, as Sweeney put, in a position to "form opinions and make decisions in the decades to come," the team has seen the game attract a much broader audience. In their testing with

Americans, Keylor said, they have seen interest from teenagers, as they expected, and even middle-aged non-gamers. Commenting on the game's cross-generational and cultural appeal, Burak added, "There is something very profound in this conflict, in trying to resolve it and in facing violence that relates to all of us, wherever and whoever we are."

Sweeney saw games like *PeaceMaker* being used in the future to teach "laws, systems, and patterns," as well as complex human interactions, that are not easily expressed in books or other non-interactive forms. With these games, he said, players will be able to "make choices they'd never actually be able to make, to see the variations in consequences, and comprehend the way some system works better than if they were passively taught it."

The plan for *PeaceMaker*, at least at the time of this writing, is to keep it freely available. Burak said that they have had some offers to commercialize the game, but they want to wait and see before making that decision. "It might be," he said, "that *PeaceMaker* will serve . . . to prove that such a game could be successful and wide spread." He added, "I personally believe that we'll see more and more serious or constructive games out there, as the industry matures."

Developing Political Games

Political games can come from personal conviction, or they can be done as contract work. Even in the latter case, however, an affinity for the policy being advocated is useful. Like the religious and art games discussed later in this chapter, political games can be very personal. Working on a project that is personally objectionable is not easy, and hardly makes sense considering the limited budgets and markets for such games.

"The budgets and markets [for political games] are certainly not as well developed as the commercial business," Bogost said, but he finds that designing and building video games that can "change the way we think about politics and education" is satisfying. He added, "If you're just making games because you like playing games, because games are cool, you're missing out on a whole lot of meaning in the world."

Designing

The design of political games is often dictated by the policies being promoted, examined, or skewered. As such, strong opinions and strong convictions are a prerequisite. Especially since, in many cases, the project must be developed and released in a sparse funding environment.

When designing serious games such as *PeaceMaker*, Burak said, the challenge is bigger than what is faced in pure entertainment. Besides having the usual constraints and risks of video game development, "you have to deal with a serious subject, the educational aspects, and bias issues." Money, in his opinion, can't be the prime motivation behind such a game. "It must be out of passion and genuine belief that it is an important thing to do."

"The message of the game is most important," Bogost said. "I make games that strive to make a point." And that is where the design begins. A large part of the design process, he said, is orienting the design of the game toward the production of certain goals outside the game. Having a definite message and goals also makes testing the effectiveness of the game during development easier. If the point of the game is not getting through to the player, he added, "then the game isn't working."

Another important part of the design, Bogost said, is the intended audience. He tries to keep the audience as broad as possible, striving to "make games that people who don't normally consider themselves gamers would be interested in." He doesn't consider his games as a wholly separate experience for the players, but as a part of the "broad media and cultural portfolio" that makes up the player's life.

Pitching

Speaking about his work on the *PeaceMaker* project, Sweeney expressed surprise that people were so open to the idea of serious games. Despite that, he said, "Until they actually see children playing and being affected by a specific game, however, they won't believe that game has value. The only way to prove an idea has merit seems to be empirically, and that requires building the game first, even in a limited state." When pitching a game like this, he said it was important to stress both the strengths and limitations of serious games as a teaching medium.

"Experts and those interested in the [Israeli-Palestinian] issue," Sweeney said, have been "very generous with their time and knowledge." These people want to see the game succeed and have been very supportive. "At the same time," he added, "the scale of the issue we're tackling makes success seem very difficult and risky, and that causes some [people] to refrain from commitment."

A willingness to help and to see such games created, however, doesn't always translate into funding. Politicians and political groups are more accustomed to asking for donations than giving them. In addition, non-profit organizations are often restricted to giving money only to other non-profit organizations. This can make it difficult for such organizations to provide direct financial assistance to developers working on for-profit projects.

However, don't underestimate the value of non-financial assistance. Universities have extensive resources, such as computers and networking. Even more importantly, they often have licenses for high-end software tools that might be out of the reach of a small, unfunded team. Beyond such tangible assets, though, organizations have often accumulated a wealth of information on their particular topic. Free access to the information they've collected and to both analyses and the analysts who processed the information can be invaluable.

Another benefit of a partnership with, or sponsorship by, an organization is use of the organization's name in other negotiations. By being able to say that you are working with or for a particular organization, your project immediately gains the credibility of that organization. This can be leveraged to create even more partnerships or secure additional sponsorships. Randy Chase, founder of Kellogg Creek Software and developer of the game *Power Politics*, credited his relationship with the national newspaper, *The Christian Science Monitor*, for attracting important partnerships like Rock the Vote.

Developing

Bogost described the typical project at Persuasive Games as having five team members working over a period of three to four months. The funding for these projects has come from corporations, non-profits, educational institutions, political policy groups, and even political candidates. Most of their budgets so far have been less than $100,000, but Bogost said that larger budgets, and hence larger games, are now being planned, and there are even some that are self-funded.

With such small budgets, it's important for developers to plan small and develop within tight technology constraints. They should leverage existing resources as much as possible, including leveraging partnerships and other relationships to get contributions. These contributions can go beyond simple money and include such valuable assets as donation of a political figure or celebrity's image or time on the project. The benefits of these are very similar to those of partnerships and sponsorships described earlier.

Since much of politics involves advertising with short, visual spots, developers may find themselves struggling to understand or be understood by the organization they're working with. "Advertising has been obsessed with the purely visual for so long," Bogost said, "it's hard for them to understand the power of procedural representation, of simulating processes instead of representing things in images." And this doesn't just apply to advertisers and political committees. "There is a general media literacy problem surrounding video games," Bogost added. Developers will need to be prepared to explain the medium of video games to their partners and interpret the goals of their partners into that new medium.

RELIGIOUS GAMES

Religious games come in two main varieties. The first is a game designed to teach religious lessons or impart religious knowledge. Such games use the doctrines and literature of the religion as a primary source of material.

The second type of religious games is those games created by religious game designers and developers. The games may not be overtly religious, and players of the games may not even be aware of the religious goals of the designers.

The first type of religious game is by far the most prevalent, and most of the religious games explored in this chapter are of that sort.

Survey of Religious Games

Religious, or faith-based, games have been around nearly as long as there have been personal computers and game consoles. Despite this, such games have never been a significant portion of the overall video game market. The growth of the contemporary Christian music market, however, shows that a niche can develop over time to become a significant market. According to the Recording Industry Association of America, Christian music in 2004 accounted for nearly 7 percent of music sales in the U.S., well over $1 billion in revenue. Though not a huge slice of the overall music market, it's still significant and represents the potential opportunity for religious games. Analysts estimate that the Christian game market is between $100–$200 million.

Underscoring this potential, Jeremy Lemer, in his March 1, 2005, article for the Columbia News Service, "Religion Goes Digital in Faith-Based Computer Games," reported that the demand for such games has grown in recent years as developers, parents, and religious leaders have become concerned with the "increasingly racy and violent content of mainstream games." "Since 1995," he wrote, "the two best-selling [faith-based] titles have sold more than 250,000 copies, and there are now around 40 different software companies developing new and increasingly sophisticated games."

N'Lightning Software, founded by Rev. Ralph Bagley, has released *Catechumen*, a first-person shooter game where the player, armed with such weapons as a lightning sword, drill sword, or explosive staff, explores the catacombs under ancient Rome, fighting Satan's minions and rescuing captured Christians. In 2001 the company followed *Catechumen*, which is reported to have sold over 80,000 copies, with *Ominous Horizons: A Paladin's Calling*, an action adventure where the player is trying to find Gutenberg's Bible, which has been stolen by Satan.

Some religiously themed products, such as *Veggie Tales* by Big Idea, have proven to be valuable licensing opportunities for their creators. *Veggie Tales*, a series of 30-minute, computer animated tales of tomatoes, cucumbers, celery, and asparagus that retell popular Bible stories and explore religious themes, has spun off a number of video games for a variety of platforms, and even a feature film. "Adventures in Odysseys" is another successful religious series, and Digital Praise Software is scheduled to release two games in 2005 based on the animated cartoon and radio show license. Moving beyond children's products, the popular religious suspense thriller, *Left Behind*, has spun off Left Behind Games and will be releasing games based on the books in 2005, as well.

Religious games cover more than Christian-themed products. Since 1982, for example, the Davka Corporation, based in Chicago, Illinois, has been producing "Judaic software." Their products have covered Jewish history, customs and traditions, the Hebrew language, and other topics of interest to Jews. *Ehud's Courage and the Cunning Blade* is one of their recent adventure games. Players have to learn and use passages from the Book of Prophets as they go through the game.

Religious Game Development Case Study—
The Interactive Parables

GraceWorks Interactive, a Christian-themed video game company founded by Tim Emmerich in 1998, has as its mission to offer video games that are better alternatives to the typical retail video game. The company calls its games "Christian Games" or "Bible-based games." The company's flagship product is *The Interactive Parables*, "a 3D interactive game that incorporates lessons on all of Jesus' lessons." The goal for the game, which Emmerich described as "a Bible-based adventure game," was to create a fun environment that also encouraged learning.

The company tried to keep the audience for the game as broad as possible, striving to appeal to "anyone interested in playing and learning." Younger children, Emmerich said, "enjoy moving around [the game world] but will need help in reading the questions if they don't know how to read yet." To help with that, the game includes a built-in text-to-speech feature. Overall, the ideal age range for the game is from 10 years old up to 18 years old. Such young people, Emmerich said, are "a group searching for many things."

The Interactive Parables was built on Academics 3D, a game system developed by Stone Engelbrite of Inspired Idea. Emmerich credited Academics 3D with making the development of the game easier, though waiting on the engine to be completed did cause some delays in the project. For future projects, though, the company expects the now completed Academics 3D engine to reduce development time to as little as a few months.

Emmerich said he learned game production and distribution hands-on, gaining experience with testing jobs. To date, GraceWorks Interactive has been fully self-funded, and volunteers have been a key component of the development team. Emmerich used a hands-on, on-the-job approach to teaching the volunteers what they needed to do, which is much like how he learned his craft. He added, "I believe that game development is something anyone can do. Obviously, if you have some skills, that helps too. But with hard work, [anyone] can persevere."

Since its release, *The Interactive Parables* has been sold at Christian retailers across the United States and via the Web. As of this writing, the game is being translated into Russian and Spanish. Much of the marketing effort has been carried out by Emmerich himself, but a few distributors for religious and family bookstores have come to the company on their own once they heard about the game.

According to Emmerich, who is also the founder of Christian Game Developers Conference (CGDC) held each year in Portland, Oregon, "the market for Christian and Bible-based games is huge and growing." The biggest challenge, he said, "is getting the market [of game players] to know that these games exist and are good alternatives to what is currently available." There is also an issue with "getting some retailers to carry the product." Religious and family bookstores have proven to be good outlets, but larger retail outlets aren't always interested in the games.

Developing Religious Games

Other than a focus on a religious message or theme, developing religious games is very similar to developing political games. Even more so than political games, however, religious games begin with the beliefs of the designer. While it's possible for the developer to be creating what is essentially a licensed product, under contract from the property owner, most religious games are conceived and developed by the same individual or organization and are self-funded.

In recent years, religious groups have become more open to video games. With few alternatives to the purely secular entertainment video games available at retail outlets, these organizations have begun considering the possibility of creating those alternatives themselves. This shift in attitude could open up additional funding opportunities.

When designing religious games, the following question must again be asked: Is the message of the game more important than the fun? Emmerich said, "Both the message and fun factor are important." He added, "In general, the message is more important. However, if the game isn't approachable and fun, no one will hear the message." Others, though, will argue that the message is all important, regardless of how fun the game might be.

Controversy tends to surround the design of religious products. No body of religious followers is homogenous, and there are differing views about how to interpret sacred texts and how to apply the lessons and commandments in the modern world. Should designers, for example, take liberties with Bible stories, adding modern elements and viewpoints to make them more accessible? Or should they adhere strictly to the original text? Creative artists of all sorts have faced these questions throughout history, and now video game designers get to wrestle with them.

This controversy is probably the main reason why so many religious games fall back on the *Jeopardy!* or *Trivial Pursuit* format of questions and answers. If the designer sticks to the literal words of the sacred text, there's little chance of offending a member of the target audience. On the other hand, such an approach severely limits the types of gameplay that can be offered.

To that end, Emmerich saw the recent growth in independent game development, funded by the developers themselves and finding players directly via the Web, as a model for religious game developers to emulate. "The whole independent game developer community," said Emmerich, "continues to grow as tools become more available. That will drive more original game ideas into the market. Christian game developers can take advantage of those tools and resources. Hopefully, we will see the quality of our titles improve tremendously."

ART GAMES

Art games are games in which the artistic expression of the game designer is more important than any other aspect (sometimes including gameplay). Like artists in other mediums, the art game designer is expressing something from within himself or herself. While the themes covered in the game may border on the political, the religious, or both, and the game may even be playable as a game in its own right, none of those aspects alone conveys the point of the game, the reason why the designer created the game.

What Are Art Games?

Art games, by their nature, tend to be very personal projects. Brody Condon, who has been involved with art games since the late 1990s, described himself as an artist and a "heavy game consumer" who eventually found himself in art school. Because of his background, he said, "It was natural . . . that I would integrate game elements into the contemporary art strategies that I was learning."

When asked how he described his projects, Condon said, "I would personally describe my work as visual arts projects that just utilize the materials and strategies of game development in various ways." He added, "The goal of my personal work tends to be a process of . . . trying to understand the links between traumatic events and fabricated memories, spiritual experience, and . . . constructed realities in contemporary culture."

Joan Leandre described a similar approach. "I'm not a game designer," she said. For her, the goal of her projects is "to hack the software in such a degree so that the response of the game later, when playing, [is] something very far from the original game objectives, a sort of software collapse." She described this as an "intervention that interrupts the natural identity of the original software."

Velvet-Strike, created by Condon and Leandre along with Anne Marie Schleiner, is a modification of the popular game, *Counter-Strike*, which is itself a modification of Valve Software's *Half-Life*. At its most basic, *Velvet-Strike* was a collection of spray paints that exploited a feature of *Counter-Strike*, which allowed players to put temporary graffiti on the walls, floors, and ceilings of buildings in the game. What was different about *Velvet-Strike* was the nature of the spray paint images: anti-war protests, social and political commentary, and even some explicit anti-American posters. Players would log in to *Counter-Strike* multiplayer servers, rush into the heaviest combat areas, and "spray" on their *Velvet-Strike* graffiti. They often died soon after as the unamused, "real" players of *Counter-Strike* expressed their opinion of the intrusions.

Leandre said she makes her games for "people interested in looking through to the other side." Though *Velvet-Strike* involved a small team, she usually works alone, with no funding. Her choice of projects comes from "daily life affinities and friendship, plus [the] sharing of essential issues and attitudes related to our contemporary world." She came out strongly against the current U.S.-led war in Iraq and against games that exemplified the conflict (such as *Counter-Strike*) or, as she saw it, exploited the war for entertainment (such as *Kuma War*, *America's Army*, and *Full Spectrum Warrior*). These games, she said, "go far beyond the idea of entertainment." She called them "propagandistic products . . . sold [from] opportunism and the enjoyment of hell on earth."

Not all art games are the same. The possible subject matter is as broad as the human experience. Some art games aim squarely for the counterculture. The Australian cyberfeminist group VNS Matrix, for example, released a game, *All New Gen*, featuring a heroine on a quest to sabotage the Big Daddy Mainframe. As she goes through the game, the player faces such opponents as the "dangerous technobimbo" Circuit Boy and bonds with "DNA sluts." *All New Gen* was created as a museum installation piece, with interactive elements built around still images and QuickTime videos.

Art games can allow the designers to deal with their own internal issues by expressing the inner turmoil of the designers just as painting and sculpture have done throughout human history. *9/11 Survivor* put the player in a 3D animated rendering of a burning World Trade Center office. The only options available to the player were to burn in the fire, jump from a window, or, if the hidden stairwell could be found, run to safety. Created as an art-class project by three students (John Brennan, Mike Caloud, and Jeff Cole) at the University of California at San Diego, *9/11 Survivor* caused a loud public outcry. Neither sensationalism nor bad taste was the goal of the designers, but the sensitive nature of the topic and the proximity to the tragedy made it hard to accept.

Art Game Case Study—*Waco Resurrection*

For their game, *Waco Resurrection*, independent developers C-Level "started out on an arty mission," Condon said, focusing on the historical content as the main objective. *Waco Resurrection*, a game about the U.S. government's siege of the Branch Davidian compound in Waco, Texas in 1993, began with a documentary focus and an intent to portray the event as accurately as possible.

FIGURE 9.5

Waco Resurrection

© C-Level. Used with Permission

"The original idea," Condon said, "was to combine strategies from documentary [film] with current game conventions to loosely deal with issues of internal security and religious fundamentalism in the [United States]." As work on the game progressed, though, their design began to shift away from strict reality. Striving to stay close to reality proved to be a mistake, Condon said, for both art production and design. The team realized that the emphasis on reality hindered "any kind of smooth sense of gameplay" and did not enhance the concept of the project. It also "went against our own chaotic intuition to embellish the scenario with fantasy elements."

As shown in Figure 9.5, the most obvious departure from total accuracy in the resulting game came with giving cult leader David Koresh magic spells. "In the end," Condon said, "I thought this kind of irresponsible relationship to the original event was more honest [and] . . . strengthened the content." It also improved the playability of the final game. Condon noted that his thrust to accurately recreate the compound and other aspects in the game adhered too close to reality and "hurt the project." He said, "While I was . . . depicting exactly where the Davidians slept, ate, and prayed, Eddo [Stern, of C-Level] had the time to go with his game-forged instincts and implement elements like spellcasting that better articulated the sensibility of the group."

The team that created *Waco Resurrection* consisted of four primary designers and contributors and another four assistants. The project took nearly five months, with only a few of the team members working on the project full time. Condon estimated the total budget for the project as between $5,000 and $10,000, mostly contributions from team members. The initial funding came from the team members, but they also received some funding from museum and event space commissions and even media art grants. Working with these groups proved useful, Condon added, because "these types of funding generally have very few intrusive requirements."

Getting traditional publisher funding for a non-commercial game like *Waco Resurrection* is almost impossible. "It's not so easy to get a publishing deal," Condon said, "if the game . . . obviously won't work at all in the traditional [retail] game market system."

This had predictable implications for *Waco Resurrection*. "The time frame for [games like *Waco Resurrection*] has to be short, as no one is getting paid." Having to work under the constraints of limited time and very limited money "caused constant organizational problems and internal personal conflicts." However, Condon went on, "this type of process allows for quick shifts in the shape of the project and total creative freedom from beginning to end."

Developing Art Games

While political games and religious games usually have the backing, or at least the understanding and approval, of organizations, special interest groups, or established religions, art games remove themselves even further from the mass culture. These games are ultimately the vision of a single developer, or, at most, the vision of a small development team trying to make a statement of its own.

Designing

Video games almost always evolve during development. This is true in the retail arena and in serious games. Usually this evolution is dictated by the constraints of the game's budget, schedule, or available technology. Condon, however, stated that art games should evolve through the entire process. "What commonly happens [in game development]," Condon said, "is an intuitive shift as the pieces evolve and find their own logic." In other words, the act of building the art game informs its design.

Leandre advised would-be art game developers to "try to see beyond the surface of playful software." Her work is almost exclusively modifications because she sees so much potential left unused in today's video games.

Pitching

Finding funding for art games can be a challenge, but it's not impossible. As Condon mentioned above, one reason why obtaining funding is a challenge is due to the non-commercial nature of the projects.

Condon described the target audience for games of this sort as "a generation of academics, artists, art viewers, and experimental game developers who grew up with games and are now demanding a more interesting use of the medium." Such an audience is open to the non-commercial, edgy ideas that retail game publishers, as well as many sources of serious game funding, would never come near. Often these are games like *9/11 Survivor* that, when noticed by the mainstream media outlets, result in outrage in the general population.

Leandre talked about the difficulty with finding a market. Just as in many other artistic practices, she said, "it takes a while for non-specialized people to understand a given cultural, technical, or social context." Software today, she added, especially video games, is still "very far from being fully understood in a conventional cultural context." This can even make showing artistic software projects in settings such as museums difficult. Museums and their visitors are "based more in a kind of curiosity than in a serious and deep understanding" of what's presented. When she does a museum installation, she said, she tries to minimize the physical aspects of the presentation. "I show software," she said.

Developing

Condon offered this advice to developers interested in creating art games:

- **Keep the time frame as short as possible.** "No one is getting paid, and motivation is easily lost without a clear deadline."

- **Don't be afraid to experiment with non-traditional methods.** "We had to randomly piece together production and distribution strategies from our own art practices as well as the industry."

- **Be flexible.** "This type of process allows for quick shifts in the shape of the project and total creative freedom from beginning to end."

An aspect of *Waco Resurrection* seldom seen in retail games is that the game was developed to be an installation piece at a museum or gallery. As art games grow as a medium, games designed as gallery installations will become more common.

"Planning a project for an installation environment," Condon said, "is fundamentally different than designing for a home computer or console." First, there is the nature of the player. Museum visitors often have a "predetermined notion" of how they look at art, which is usually passive. In order to convince them to actually sit down and play the game, the game's "interface has to be even more simple (or just more interesting) than normal."

Also, the gameplay in an installation piece should focus on shorter scenarios with an emphasis on providing what Condon called a "spectator projection." That is, it needs to be an experience that can be viewed by visitors who do not want to sit down and play. Finally, the developer has to balance attention-grabbing techniques against the tendency of art viewers to ignore anything they consider overly commercial. "Smart content," Condon said, "then an interesting visual experience, has to play a key role at all times."

Installation pieces have to provide the software, with all resources, and the hardware to run it on. The cost of the hardware can be kept down, depending on the specifications of the particular project and the underlying software. However, a special license for third-party software, particularly games, might need to be purchased. Games in particular are usually licensed for private play. Public display, even in a non-profit museum setting, is typically not available from a game purchased at retail. Developers should contact the publisher of the game to get the necessary permission.

"The most obvious prediction," said Condon when asked about the future of art games, "is that a game production and distribution system will eventually show up which mimics the history of independent and experimental film and video." Independent game development, mentioned earlier by Emmerich, again provides an example that can be followed.

CONCLUSION

"Believe in something," Bogost said. That's the first step to making a political game, a religious game, or an art game. These are personal games. They require the designer to look inside, find something to say, and then have the guts to say it in a game. Game developers, he said, "need to have meaningful connections with people and ideas and a drive to express them."

The retail video game publishers have a simple agenda: They want to make money. They aren't an evil empire or against innovation or personal expression. They just want to turn a profit. A big profit. The games talked about in this chapter, and indeed in many of the previous chapters, aren't even on the publishers' radars. In many cases, the profit potential just isn't there, at least not yet.

Most game developers, though, are more into the fun and excitement of creating video games, of building an experience that is enjoyed and shared by players. Money, except as a way to pay the bills, doesn't really enter into the equation. If game developers were only interested in money, they would be using their skills in other industries, like corporate IT or the Hollywood dream factories, where the pay level is higher, the benefits are better, and the hours are shorter.

Political games, religious games, and art games, or a combination of some or all of these, represent an opportunity for game developers to create something that matters more to them as individuals, a personal statement instead of a shipping stock unit.

Not every game developer is going to be interested in doing personal and/or non-commercial work. However, even for those with an eye on the possible financial return, stories like that of GraceWorks Interactive, where the company has been able to create a game that sells within the intended market on a very small budget, should be a clue to how it can be done. A project can be both personal and potentially profitable.

FINAL THOUGHTS

Over the past few years there has been a lot of talk within the video game industry about its "growing up" and becoming a mature industry. The industry is maturing not only in the subject matter presented in popular video games, but also in the way those games are designed, developed, distributed, and played.

A key sign of this growing maturity is the broadening audience of game players. No longer the domain of young men and children, video games have reached across ethnic and cultural boundaries and around the world to men, women, and children of all ages. As computers and computing technology have become more powerful and less expensive, they have become increasingly pervasive. Video games have moved into the mainstream and are an undeniable part of mass culture.

Video games are poised to become more relevant, more responsible, and more important within the wider world than ever before. To put it in other words, the time has come for video games to get serious.

Serious games are still in the process of defining themselves within the spectrum of video games. From vehicle simulators to specialized policy games, entirely new forms of serious game have already begun to evolve, utilizing newly created video game technology to form games and products that weren't feasible—or possibly even imagined—only a decade ago.

Thus the future of serious games is one of exploration. It encourages a sifting of possibilities while defining both the strengths and weaknesses of this new medium. New platforms, like cell phones and PDAs, and new techniques, like pervasive games and social simulations, are all coming together with existing technology to find new ways to train so many people. With the aid of serious games, soldiers will defend our country and policymakers will weigh difficult choices. First responders and doctors will save lives, and corporate trainers will guide employees to higher levels of achievement. Students will gain a better understanding about the world and find innovative means of expression. Moreover, serious games can help both sides of a contentious issue to understand each other. Certainly, all aspects of our future will be changed by serious games.

Serious games won't replace teachers, therapists, or other training and education professionals. Instead, these new games will be a new tool in the educational toolbox, one with the potential to alter the teaching and training paradigm. Serious games offer students and trainees the motivation to play and to learn, the engagement with the subject matter in a relevant context, and an environment that is under the complete control of the teacher.

So where do we go from here? In the survey we conducted for this book (see survey result 10.1), we asked the respondents what they saw as the main issues that need to be addressed to improve the state of serious games. Several of these issues, like improved artificial intelligence (AI) and improved NPC behavior, improved simulation of real-world physics, and a better distribution model, are important even for entertainment video games. Others, like research into the effectiveness of serious games, more public funding, and better tools for testing and assessment, are unique to serious games.

SERIOUS GAMES SURVEY RESULT 10.1

Question: What issue(s) do you think need to be addressed to improve the state of serious games?

- More research into the effectiveness of serious games

- Improved artificial intelligence (AI) and non-player character (NPC) behavior

- Improved low-cost content creation tools and development tools, as well as more open-source options

- More private and commercial funding of research and projects

- More public funding of research and projects

- Better testing and assessment tools

- Improved real-world physics simulation

- More commercial off-the-shelf (COTS) alternatives

- Better distribution models

- Improved logging and replay features

- Pedagogy incorporating serious games

- Wider acceptance of serious games for teaching and training

---

More research into the effectiveness of serious games for teaching, training, and informing is necessary not only to convince educators and trainers that such games should be used, but also to help more game developers and game players see the full potential of their favorite medium. Game developers need to be shown that the games they create are significant outside the realm of pure entertainment. Game players as well need to be shown that what they've learned in the simulated world of games can be put to good use in the real world.

In Conclusion

Serious games have been around for decades but have seldom received much attention from the greater part of the video game development industry. As games mature as a medium of expression, they become an even more important part of mainstream culture. Their use in education (and training, and physical therapy, and psychotherapy, and more) is inevitable.

There is still a lot of research that must be completed. We need to uncover new ways to use serious games and the best way to design these applications. However, there can be little doubt that serious games represent one of the most significant trends in video game development since the move into the third dimension.

Part

3

Appendixes

RESOURCES

The growth in serious games has led to new conferences and associations and also to a new awareness of some conferences and organizations that have existed for years. The following lists are just a sampling of the resources available to people interested in developing serious games. The attention to serious games is certain to continue, so be on the lookout for sessions or talks at universities and local IGDA chapters.

CONFERENCES

Serious Games Summit D.C.

(www.seriousgamessummit.com)

Produced by the CMP Game Group, the Serious Games Summit D.C. held in Washington, D.C. seeks to highlight "interactive solutions for shared challenges" in the following non-entertainment fields: government, healthcare, the military, corporate, first responders, and science. While geared toward educating project managers rather than game developers, there are still worthwhile opportunities for developers, especially in regard to networking. An abbreviated version of the Serious Games Summit, which is targeted toward game developers, occurs before the annual Game Developers Conference (GDC).

G.A.M.E.S. Synergy Summit

(www.synergysummit.com/)

The G.A.M.E.S. Synergy Summit, held in Orlando, Florida, fosters collaboration between the following industries: government, academia, the military, entertainment, and simulation (hence, G.A.M.E.S.). Since Orlando is home to a large training and simulation community, many of the sessions cater toward people actively engaged in government projects. Of particular note are the "bridge" sessions, which help companies find effective ways to bridge the gap between the entertainment industry and government agencies.

The Interservice/Industry Training, Simulation, and Education Conference (I/ITSEC)

(www.iitsec.org/)

With delegates from government agencies of various countries in attendance, the Interservice/Industry Training, Simulation, and Education Conference, more familiarly known as I/ITSEC, is the government contractor's equivalent of the Electronic Entertainment Expo (E3). Held in Orlando, Florida, the conference focuses on improving training and education programs among numerous divisions of the armed services, government agencies, academia, and industry.

Visuals and Simulation Technology Conference and Exhibition (ViSTech)

(www.halldale.com/vistech/)

The Visuals and Simulation Technology Conference and Exhibition, or ViSTech, which made its debut June 2005 in Orlando, Florida, is directed toward commercial and military designers, manufacturers, and users of visual system technology. The conference covers the use of game technology in military and government applications.

Education Arcade, Games in Education Conference
(www.educationarcade.org/)

Held in Los Angeles, California, in conjunction with the Electronic Entertainment Expo (E3), the Education Arcade explores issues and new frontiers in the development, use, and marketing of educational games. By leveraging efforts from the game industry and university partners, the initiative seeks to encourage research and development of educational games.

Games, Learning, and Society Conference
(www.glsconference.org)

The Games, Learning, and Society Conference (GLS) in Madison, Wisconsin, explores the potential of games in learning and social change. Academics, game designers, and educators discuss research into educational games as well as the pervasive impact of games on popular culture.

Video Game/Entertainment Industry Technology and Medicine Conference
(www.gamenmed.com/)

Held in California, the Video Game/Entertainment Industry Technology and Medicine Conference (VEITMC) fosters shared collaboration between the diverse fields of cinema effects, video games, military applications, and medicine. Topics include all aspects of games in healthcare: the effects of games, medical simulations, emergency care, and mental health.

Games for Health
(www.gamesforhealth.org/events.html)

Produced by the Serious Games Initiative, the Games for Health Conference explores the role of games and game technologies in healthcare applications and policy. The conference brings together researchers, medical professionals, and game developers to discuss how games can improve health education, training, service, and administration.

Medicine Meets Virtual Reality
(www.nextmed.com/mmvr_virtual_reality.html)

Held in Long Beach, California, Medicine Meets Virtual Reality (MMVR) features presentations on virtual reality tools for clinical diagnosis and therapy, medical training simulations, and patient care. It is intended for healthcare professionals, healthcare educators, military medical specialists, computer technologists, and biomedical futurists.

Cyber Therapy Conference
(www.interactivemediainstitute.com/conference2005.org/index.htm)

Held in Switzerland, the Cyber Therapy Conference is the largest conference focusing on cutting-edge technologies used in mental health, rehabilitation, disabilities, medical training, and health education. Technologies discussed include virtual reality, video games, robotics, and the Internet.

Future Play
(www.futureplay.org)

The goal of the Future Play Conference is to promote experimental game design, advance serious game efforts, and nurture new talent within the game community. The FuturePlay Game Exhibition and Competition showcases games from academics, students, independent, and experimental game developers.

Free Play: Next Wave Independent Game Developers Conference
(www.nextwave.org.au/freeplay/)

Held in Australia in conjunction with the Next Wave Festival, Free Play features experimental and independent game development. Developed by indie game developers for indie game developers, the conference showcases art games in addition to more business-oriented independent game development issues.

Christian Game Developers Conference
(www.cgdc.org/)

The Christian Game Developers Conference, held in Portland, Oregon, is the only conference dedicated to encouraging and integrating Christian principles in games. Session topics cover the nuts and bolts of the game industry with a Christian twist, like the merits of free will or predestination in game design.

ORGANIZATIONS

International Simulation and Gaming Association (ISAGA)
(www.isaga.info/)

ISAGA and its affiliates, like the North American Simulation and Gaming Association (NASAGA, www.nasaga.org), represent scientists developing and/or using simulation or gaming technologies. ISAGA has its own annual conference and its official publication, *Simulation and Gaming: An Interdisciplinary Journal of Theory, Practice and Research* (www.unice.fr/sg/).

The American Society of Trainers and Developers (ASTD)
(www.astd.org/astd)

ASTD is the world's largest association for corporate trainers and educators. Its membership includes those from academia, government agencies, multinational businesses, and consulting firms. ASTD has its own annual conference, local chapters, and a publication called *Training & Development* (www.astd.org/astd/publications/td_magazine).

Digital Games Research Association (DiGRA)
(www.digra.org/)

DiGRA is an international association for academics and game researchers. It delves into game theory as well as the social impact of games. DiGRA has its own annual conference.

International Association of Games Education Research (IAGER)
(www.iager.org/)

A new organization, IAGER focuses on educational game research and its practical integration into the classroom. Membership is open to game researchers, educators, and game developers. IAGER is launching its own publication, *Journal of Game Education and Research*, and intends to hold an annual conference.

Games for Change (G4C)
(www.seriousgames.org/gamesforchange/)

An activist offshoot of the Serious Games Initiative, Games for Change addresses the interest of non-profit organizations in games. With local and international chapters, special seminars, and frequent appearances at related conferences, the group promotes the use of games to further organization aims and bring about societal change. Games For Change has an annual conference.

Christian Game Developers Foundation (CGDF)
(www.cgdf.org/)

Founded by Christian game developers, CGDF assists Christian game developers and also provides parental warnings about objectionable games on the market. Its interest is to encourage the development of alternatives to violent or overly sexual mainstream games.

CONTESTS

Hidden Agenda

(www.hiddenagenda.com/)

Sponsored by the Liemandt Foundation, Hidden Agenda is a competition for aspiring game developers enrolled in college who want to further "stealth education" at the middle school level. The winner receives the $25,000 grand prize.

WEB SITES

Serious Games Initiative (www.seriousgames.org)

Department of Defense Game Developers' Community (www.dodgamecommunity.com/index.php)

Games For Health (www.gamesforhealth.org)

Water Cooler Games—video games with an agenda (www.watercoolergames.org)

artFUTURE (www.artfuture.com)

Christian Gaming (www.christiangaming.com)

PUBLICATIONS

Military Simulation & Training (http://mst.at-events.com)

Training & Simulation Journal (www.TSJonline.com)

Training (www.trainingmag.com)

eLearn Magazine (www.eLearnMag.org)

Game Developer (www.gdmag.com/homepage.htm)

Serious Games Survey Results

As part of the research for this book, in the spring of 2005 we conducted a short survey of developers, educators, and researchers involved or interested in serious games. The survey was posted on a handful of serious games information sites and e-mailing lists, and was announced at the G.A.M.E.S. Synergy Summit and the Serious Games Summit at the Game Developers Conference.

A total of 63 respondents completed the survey, representing a wide spectrum. As the results demonstrate, the respondents came from game development, education, business, government and military, healthcare, and more.

SURVEY NOTES

The total responses to each question are noted, as well as the tally of each particular answer. These have been converted to percentages to make the information easier to read.

During the review and summarizing process, some of the questions were deemed irrelevant (for example, "Why do you attend conferences?") and those were removed from the results.

Questions that asked freeform or "short answer" questions have been summarized for brevity, with similar responses combined.

Demographic Information

Job Titles of Respondents

President (4)

Game Designer (3)

Assistant Professor (2)

Chief Executive Officer (2)

Managing Director (2)

Managing Partner (2)

PhD Candidate (2)

Program Manager (2)

Researcher (2)

Administrator

Business Developer

Character Designer

Consulting Analyst

Creator of Learning Environments

Chief Technology Officer

Director, Institute for New Media Studies

Director of Development

Director of Serious Games

Freelance

Freelance Designer/Producer

Instructional Designer/Project Manager

Lead Engineer

Lead Programmer

Learning Technologist

Manager, New Business Development

Media Projects Coordinator

Multimedia Developer

Organization and Culture Developer

Owner

Producer/Designer/Consultant

Professor and Communications Technology Lab Director

Project Engineer

Project Lead

Project Manager

Research Assistant

Research Associate

Second Year Master's Student

Senior Application Developer

Senior Designer

Senior Integrator

Software Developer

Software Engineer

Spencer Research Fellow (and Graduate Student)

Student

Teacher

Training and Project Manager

Webmaster/Editor

Total   61 responses

Industries

66.67% (42) Game Development

49.21% (31) Education/Training

30.16% (19) Business

15.87% (10) Student

14.29% (9) Military

7.94% (5) Healthcare

7.94% (5) Government Agency

6.35% (4) Non-profit

3.17% (2) Consulting

3.17% (2) Mental Health

3.17% (2) Emergency/First Response

3.17% (2) Research

1.59% (1) Computer/Technology

4.76% (3) Other

Total   63 responses

Serious Game Projects

How many serious games projects have you been involved with, overseen, or worked on?

4.76% (3) 0

71.43% (45) 1–5

9.52% (6) 6–10

7.94% (5) 11–50

6.35% (4) 50+

Total   63 responses

What is/was your role on your most recent serious games project?

47.62% (30)   Developer, Primary Contractor

44.44% (28)   Designer

36.51% (23)   Producer

23.81% (15)   Consultant

17.46% (11)   Developer, Subcontractor

3.17% (2)   Sponsor

1.56% (1)   Other

Total   63 responses

What is/was the budget of your most recent serious games project?

18.03% (11) $0–$5000

8.20% (5) $5001–$10,000

9.84% (6) $10,001–$50,000

9.84% (6) $50,001–$100,000

26.23% (16) $100,001–$500,000

11.48% (7) $500,001–$1,000,000

14.75% (9) $1,000,001–$10,000,000

1.64% (1) $10,000,000+

Total   61 responses

What is/was the team size of your most recent serious games project?

73.77% (45)   1–10

18.03% (11)   11–25

6.56% (4)   26–50

1.64% (1)   51–100

Total   61 responses

What is/was the (projected) timeframe of your most recent serious games project?

28.33% (17)   1–6 months

35.00% (21)   6 months–1 year

21.67% (13)   1–2 years

13.33% (8)   3–5 years

1.67% (1)   5+ years

Total   60 responses

If you are a developer, how long did it take to go from initial pitch to signed contract?

48.89% (22)   1–3 months

24.44% (11)   4–6 months

11.11% (5)   6 months–1 year

11.11% (5)   1–2 years

4.44% (2)   2+ years

Total   45 responses

If you are a producer or sponsor, how long did it take you to find a developer?

86.96% (20)   1–3 months

4.35% (1)   4–6 months

4.35% (1)   6 months–1 year

4.35% (1)   2+ years

Total   23 responses

How many bids/proposals do you generally receive?

86.67% (26)   1–5

13.33% (4)   6–10

Total   30 responses

Who has been the target audience(s) of your serious games projects?

53.97% (34)   Students (any level)

47.62% (30)   General public

26.98% (17)   Corporate management and/or executives

23.40% (16)   Education professionals

23.81% (15)   Government personnel

23.81% (15)   Healthcare professionals

22.22% (14)   Corporate employees

17.46% (11)   Military personnel

7.94% (5)   Healthcare patients (including Mental Health)

7.94% (5)   Emergency Medical Personnel/First Responders

4.76% (3)   Other

1.59% (1)   Activists

Total   63 responses

What type of serious game was your most recent project?

63.49% (40)   Simulation/Training

33.33% (21)   Judgmental/Decision-making

33.33% (21)   Instructional/Educational

6.35% (4)   Policy

6.35% (4)   Political/Protest

4.76% (3)   Art

1.59% (1)   Religious

1.59% (1)   Entertainment

3.17% (2)   Other

Total   63 responses

Have you ever sponsored or authored a SBIR/STTR, BAA, or similar government RFP?

83.61% (51)   No

16.39% (10)   Yes

Total   61 responses

Have you ever worked on a SBIR/STTR, BAA, or similar government-funded project?

75.00% (45)   No

25.00% (15)   Yes

Total   60 responses

If you are a game developer, how has working on a serious game project differed from working on a retail game project?

The 21 responses to this optional question ranged from "not much different" to "utterly different." Most of the responses, though, landed in the middle of that range, pointing out what they saw as new or unexpected. After all, as one respondent wrote, "It's contract work," so most of the differences are just the normal differences between clients.

There were a few comments about the clients being unfamiliar with game design and development, such as, "They know they want a game, but don't know much about the process." In some cases, though, the client proved to be more demanding and less understanding of game development industry conventions.

Other responses included

- There is a higher ratio of simulation to game, with more interaction with outside experts, and the basis for the gameplay isn't always obvious.

- There is less of an emphasis on graphics, but an increased emphasis on the process.

- The client exercises much more control over the game's design and content than most publishers do.

- There are more standards, policies, and documentation requirements to be dealt with.

- The market is smaller and so are the budgets.

- The release date is determined by the client, not seasonal dates, like Christmas.

If you are a game developer, how many years of experience do you have in the game industry?

12.00% (6)   < 1 year

26.00% (13)   1–2 years

28.00% (14)   3–5 years

8.00% (4)   6–10 years

12.00% (6)   11–20 years

14.00% (7)   21+ years

Total   50 responses

How many years have you been involved with serious game development?

11.48% (7)   < 1 year

37.70% (23)   1–2 years

21.31% (13)   3–5 years

13.11% (8)   6–10 years

9.84% (6)   11–20 years

6.56% (4)   21+ years

Total   61 responses

If you are a developer, do you only develop serious games?

62.50% (35)   No

37.50% (21)   Yes

Total   56 responses

If not, do you see much overlap between your entertainment and serious game projects?

80.00% (24)   Yes

20.00% (6)   No

Total   30 responses

Did you need a security clearance to work on your most recent serious game project?

85.96% (49)   No

14.04% (8)   Yes

Total   57 responses

If yes, what level?

25.00% (2)   Confidential

50.00% (4)   Secret

25.00% (2)   Top Secret

Total   8 responses

SERIOUS GAMES—THE FUTURE

What is your goal with/for serious games?

80.95% (51)   Education

65.08% (41)   Training

50.79% (32)   Informing

22.22% (14)   Activism

20.63% (13)   Other

Total   63 responses

Among the "Other" responses were a few notable entries:

- Promoting healthier living and deeper thinking
- Improved realism in simulations, research
- Sharing of best practices in industry and education
- Policy change
- Greater emotional involvement in games
- Fun

What issue(s) do you think needs to be addressed to improve the state of serious games?

73.02% (49)   More research into the effectiveness of serious games, pedagogy using serious games

49.21% (32)   Improved Artificial Intelligence (AI) and Non-Player Character (NPC) behavior

42.86% (30)   Improved content creation tools, more open-source options

44.44% (30)   More private/commercial funding of research and projects

41.27% (29)   More public funding of research and projects

44.44% (29)   Better testing/assessment tools

30.16% (19)   Real-world physics simulation

26.98% (17)   More commercial, off-the-shelf (COTS) alternatives

20.63% (14)   Better distribution model

19.05% (12)   Improved logging/replay features

20.63% (1)   Other

Total   63 responses

Do you think serious games will become a standard part of an education/training curriculum?

95.24% (60)   Yes

4.76% (3)   No

Total   63 responses

Why or why not?

This question evoked 48 responses, some of them rather long. Many of them presented the same basic arguments, though, so we've summarized them.

"Yes, Why?" responses were as follows:

- Because learning through play is "incredibly effective and motivating," and offers students the opportunity to "experientially engage with course materials" or to learn by doing.

- Because serious games offer a safe and inexpensive training environment, an alternative to expensive real-world exercises.

- Because the current generation is used to video games and TV, not books or lectures. If you could have fun while learning, why wouldn't you? And these video game players will eventually be the teachers.

- Because serious games align with the current constructivist approach to teaching.

- Because there is money to be made with serious games.

- Eventually serious games will be a standard part of education, though probably not in the near future.

Not a lot of surprises there.

"No, Why not?" responses were as follows:

- Because public interest in and acceptance of serious games is at too low a level.
- Because some people respond very negatively to even the idea of a "game" having value.

How do you rate the importance of the "element of fun" in serious games?

33.33% (21)	5 Very important
47.62% (30)	4
15.87% (10)	3 Useful, but not a primary goal
3.17% (2)	2
0.00% (0)	1 Not important

Total   63 responses

CONFERENCES

What related conferences do you attend or have you attended?

61.90% (39)	Game Developers Conference (GDC)
31.75% (20)	E3
30.16% (19)	Serious Games Summit, D.C.
22.22% (14)	Serious Games Summit, at GDC
15.87% (10)	I/ITSEC
14.29% (9)	Education Arcade

9.52% (6)   G.A.M.E.S. Synergy Summit, Orlando, FL

3.17% (2)   Cyber Therapy

3.17% (2)   Games for Health

3.17% (2)   Digital Games Research Association (DiGRA)

3.17% (2)   North American Simulation and Gaming Association (NASAGA)

1.59% (1)   American Medical Informatics Association (AMIA) annual symposium

1.59% (1)   Games, Learning, and Society Conference

1.59% (1)   International Conference on Quantum Communication, Measurement, and Computing

1.59% (1)   State of Play

1.59% (1)   System Dynamics Society

1.59% (1)   Systems Thinking in Action

15.87% (10)   Other

Total   63 responses

Do you feel like there is a single place to find serious game developers?

83.87% (52)   No

16.13% (10)   Yes

Total   62 responses

Do you feel like there is a single place to pitch serious game ideas (to find funding)?

96.72% (59)   No

3.28% (2)   Yes

Total   61 responses

How did you get involved with serious games?

A number of the 37 responses to this optional question were from game industry veterans who hadn't originally planned to create serious games. Either their entertainment game caught the attention of government or military trainers looking for a new solution to an old problem, or they realized that the retail game industry wasn't going to pursue a particular type of simulation that they enjoyed playing. Quite a few others came from the other direction. They worked for the military, government, or education creating simulations and found themselves building games or game-like software.

Here is a summary of the responses:

- I/my company was approached by the government/military/a corporation about using my/our current game for training.

- I/my company decided to pursue serious games when I/it decided to leverage my/its expertise in games/simulations for training soldiers/first responders/salespeople.

- I began by designing/building games for my children/students/myself.

- I saw the opportunity for serious games at the Serious Games Summit/ G.A.M.E.S. Synergy Summit/other conference.

- My background in multimedia and healthcare/research/education/ communication proved a good combination for serious games.

APPENDIX C

BIBLIOGRAPHY

Abt, Clark C. *Serious Games.* Lanham, MD: University Press of America, 1987. (Reprint. Originally published: New York: Viking Press, 1970.)

Aldrich, Clark. *Simulations and the Future of Learning.* San Francisco, CA: Pfeiffer, 2004.

Bartholomew LK, Shegog R, Parcel GS, Gold RS, Fernandez M, Czyzewski DI, Sockrider MM, Berlin N. "Watch, Discover, Think, and Act: A Model for Patient Education Program Development." *Patient Education and Counseling* 2000; 39 (2-3): 253-268.

Bean, Michael. "What Makes a Simulation Fun?" Forio Business Simulations, http://www.forio.com/fun_20010702.htm.

Beck, John C. and Mitchell Wade. *Got Game: How the Gamer Generation Is Reshaping Business Forever.* Boston, MA: Harvard Business School Press, 2004.

Boehle, Sarah. "Simulations: The Next Generation of E-learning." *Training.* March 2005.

Carolipio, Redmond. "Video Games, Fitness, Medicine Team Up." *San Bernardino County Sun.* May 25, 2005.

Clark, Brian L. "Targeting the DHS." *Inc.* May 2005: 44-46.

Davis, Matthew. "Christians Purge Video Game Demons." *BBC News*. May 24, 2005.

Dingfelder, S. "Psychologist-Designed Game Linked to Improvements in Children's Diets." *APA Monitor on Psychology*. September 2004. Volume 35, No. 8.

Doyle, Mark. "Software Re-Enacts Rwanda Genocide." *BBC News*, January 20, 2005.

Dunnigan, James F. *The Complete Wargames Handbook, Revised Edition.* New York, NY: Quill, 1992.

Frank, Diane and Dibya Sarkar. "Regional Approaches Get Thumbs Up." *Federal Computer Week*. October 18, 2004. Volume 18, No. 37: 58-59.

Gee, James Paul. *What Video Games Have to Teach Us About Learning and Literacy*. New York, NY: Palgrave Macmillan, 2003.

Gill, Jennifer. "Gender Issues." *Inc.* April 2005: 38-40.

Golze, Benjamin. "Spot On: Christian Game Makers Rise to New Heights." *GameSpot*. July 6, 2004.

High, Kamau. "How Playing Power Drives Lessons Home." *Financial Times*. September 8, 2004: 9.

Huizinga, Johan. *Homo Ludens*. Boston, MA: The Beacon Press, 1955.

Iverson, Kathleen M. *E-learning games: Interactive Learning Strategies for Digital Delivery*. Upper Saddle River, NJ: Pearson Prentice Hall, 2005.

Jenkins, Henry and Kurt Squire. "Games Get Serious 2.0." *Computer Games*. June 2005.

Kirriemuir, John. "A Survey of COTS Games Used in Education." Presentation at the Serious Games Summit/Game Developers Conference, March 2005.

Kitfield, James. "On the Virtual Battlefield." *Government Executive*. August 1999.

Laramée, François Dominic. *Secrets of the Game Business, Second Edition*. Hingham, MA: Charles River Media, 2005.

Lemer, Jeremy. "Religion Goes Digital in Faith-Based Computer Games." *Columbia News Service*. March 1, 2005.

Liddane, Lisa. "Acting Out: Kids Get into the Game." *Orange County Register*. February 26, 2005.

Mankin, Eric. "Game Plan." *USC Trojan Family Magazine*. Summer 2005: 29-37.

Mcintosh, John. "Sci-fi Medicine." *Remedy*. Summer 2005: 63-70.

"Computer Technology in the Public School Classroom: Teacher Perspectives." National Center for Education Statistics, U.S. Department of Education Institute, March 2005.

Perla, Peter P. *The Art of Wargaming*. Annapolis, MD: Naval Institute Press, 1990.

Peters, Tom. *Re-imagine!* London: Dorling Kindersley, 2003.

Phillips, Stephen. "Recruiting Young People with Free Battle Games." *Financial Times*. August 7, 2002.

Prensky, Marc. *Digital Game-Based Learning*. New York, NY: McGraw-Hill, 2001.

Rich, Frank. "We'll Win This War—on '24'" *New York Times*. January 6, 2005.

Robar, Jason. "Multiplayer Technology: A Primer." *Military Simulation & Training*. December 2004.

Robel, Michael K. "The Difference Between Military & Civilian Wargames." http://www.strategypage.com/wargames/articles/wargame_articles_ 2004919231.asp.

Rosser, J.C. Jr., P.J. Lynch, L.A. Haskamp, A. Yalif, D.A. Gentile, and L. Giammaria. *Are Video Game Players Better at Laparoscopic Surgery?* Presentation at the Medicine Meets Virtual Reality Conference, Newport Beach, CA, 2004.

Salen, Katie and Eric Zimmerman. *Rules of Play.* Cambridge, MA: The MIT Press, 2004.

Saltzman, Marc. "Winners and Snoozers," *AARP The Magazine.* March/April 2005: 16.

Sawyer, Ben. "Getting Serious about New Opportunities." http://www.gamasutra.com/features/20041015/sawyer_01.shtml.

Schrage, Michael. *Serious Play: How the World's Best Companies Simulate to Innovate.* Boston MA: Harvard Business School Press, 2000.

Sheffield, Brandon. "Breaking the Waves." *Game Developer.* February 2005: 25-26.

Silberman, Steve. "The War Room." *Wired.* Issue 12; September 9, 2004.

Slagle, Matt. "Army Unveils New Ultra-Real Simulation." Associated Press, December 20, 2004.

Smith, Wes. "Hurt Soldiers Still Help Country—Virtually." *Orlando Sentinel.* March 11, 2005.

Squire, Kurt. "What Happens When Games Go into Any Classroom Situation?" Presentation at the Serious Games Summit, Washington, D.C., October 2004.

Strassman, Mark. " Uncle Sam Wants Video Gamers." *CBS Evening News.* February 8, 2005.

Szita, Jane. "Cyberdykes R Us." *Wired*. Issue 3; September 1995.

Taleb, Nassim Nicholas. "Learning to Expect the Unexpected." *New York Times*. April 8, 2004.

Terdiman, Daniel. "Second Life Teaches Life Lessons." *Wired*. April 06, 2005.

Thibault, Aaron. "Assessment and the Future of Fluid Learning Environments." Presentation at the Serious Games Summit, Washington, D.C., October 2004.

Thompson, Clive. "The Making of an XBox Warrior." *New York Times*. August 22, 2004.

Tiboni, Frank. "DARPA Expands Robot Plane Work." *Federal Computer Week*. Volume 18, No. 37; October 18, 2004: 14.

Vargas, Jose Antonio. "Problems You Can Shake a Joystick At." *Washington Post*. October 18, 2004: A1, A10.

Wolf, Mark J. *The Medium of the Video Game*. Austin, TX: University of Texas Press, 2002.

Zeller, Shawn. "Training Games." *Government Executive*. January 2005.

GLOSSARY

Advergames. A blend of advertising and gaming, advergames are games that promote a specific product or service.

After-Action Review (AAR). In the military, the phase of mission training that provides both commanders and personnel with direct feedback about the success (or failure) of the mission.

Art Games. Games where the artistic expression of the game designer is more important than any other aspect (sometimes including gameplay).

Artificial Intelligence (AI). AI covers both the research of making computers think like humans and the use of various techniques to simulate thinking in video game opponents.

Assessment. Assessment is the use of tests, examinations, questionnaires, surveys, and other sources to draw inferences about how much of a lesson or other presented material was understood and retained by students.

Biofeedback Game. A game that uses the player's physiological responses as a means to affect gameplay. For instance, a player in a biofeedback game may be able to increase a car's speed by becoming less tense.

Black Swan. A "black swan" is an event that not only wasn't predicted, but is so far outside the realm of what's expected that it's possible it *couldn't* have been predicted.

Broad Agency Announcements (BAAs). An announcement sent out by a federal agency outlining its general research interests, specifying the general terms and conditions under which an award may be made, and inviting proposals from interested vendors.

Coaching Mode. Coaching mode allows instructors to interact with the player. Options range from simple instruction (via voice chat or typed text) to changing the effect of player decisions or even changing parts of the simulation or situation while it's running.

Commercial Off-the-Shelf Games (COTS). Games and development tools that are available to purchase from third parties.

Constructivism. An educational philosophy that stresses active learning by constructing ideas and relationships through experimentation.

Distraction Therapy. Distraction therapy helps patients, especially children, focus on something else during painful medical procedures.

Edutainment. A category of educational games and software initially promoted as "education through entertainment."

E-learning. A type of computer-assisted instruction focusing on Web-based content and delivery.

Exergaming. Also known as exertainment or fitness gaming, exergaming is the combination of exercise equipment or aerobic workout regimens with computer gaming.

Faith-Based Game. A religiously themed product or a game that reflects the spiritual ideals of the game developer.

Federal Acquisition Regulations (FARs). The policies and procedures for procurements (contracts) by and for the use of federal agencies, including the solicitation and selection of sources, award of contracts, contract financing, contract performance and administration, and technical and management functions related to contracts.

First-Person Shooter (FPS). A subgenre of video games whereby players view the game world from a first-person perspective, usually over the barrel of a gun or other weapon.

First Responders. First responders are any of the emergency personnel that would normally be first to respond to any emergency situation, whether man-made or natural. These include emergency medical technicians, firefighters, and police officers.

Intellectual Property (IP). Intellectual property is the group of legal rights to things people create or invent, including patent, copyright, trademark, and trade secret rights.

Massively Multiplayer Online Games (MMOGs). MMOGs are multiplayer computer games that feature a persistent game world in which thousands of players can interact with each other or with NPCs at any given time.

Modding. "Modding" is modifying an existing game. These user modifications can range from minor tweaking to the addition of new content to "total conversions" that change the game significantly.

Non-Disclosure Agreement (NDA). An NDA is an agreement between two parties that states that one cannot disclose designated company information and trade secrets.

Non-Governmental Organization (NGO). Non-profit groups or associations created to pursue particular social objectives (such as education about a disease) or serve particular constituencies (such as indigenous peoples).

Non-Player Characters (NPCs). Characters in computer games that players can interact with but cannot control.

Observer Mode. Observer mode allows uninvolved players to "observe" the game while it is being played by someone else.

Operations Research (OR). A type of systems analysis that brings modern science, mathematics, and statistics to bear on solving a particular problem.

Pedagogy. The science (or art) of teaching and teaching methods.

Pilot. A pilot is the first playable demo of a game shown to a client.

Political Game. Political games promote or come out against particular government policy positions or aspects of government.

Psychometrics. The field of measuring mental capabilities, such as thinking and knowledge.

Real-Time Strategy Game (RTS). A computer game genre in which players must make strategic decisions while facing ever-changing situations in a simulation that updates in "real time."

Recognition Prime Decision Making (RPD). RPD is a model for how experts make decisions under stressful situations. The goal of RPD training is to teach how to make a "good" decision immediately instead of waiting (possibly until it's too late) to come up with the "best" decision.

Request for Proposal (RFP). Formal invitations issued by businesses or government agencies requesting interested vendors to submit written proposals meeting a particular set of requirements. Interested vendors respond with a description of the techniques they would employ to meet the posted requirements, a plan of work, and a detailed budget for the project.

Role-Playing Game (RPG). A game genre in which players assume fictional roles within a shared story. Characters are created based on various attributes that advance or change as the player proceeds through the game.

Section 508. An amendment to the Rehabilitation Act of 1973. Section 508 requires that the federal government acquire only electronic and information technology goods and services that provide for access by people with disabilities.

Security Clearance. A clearance given to those people whom the government, military, or another organization deems trustworthy enough to have access to sensitive or classified material.

Simulation. An abstraction of some element or elements of physical reality. Sometimes simulations are highly accurate reproductions of natural processes, and, other times simulations are simplified to emphasize relationships between certain factors.

Small Business Innovation Research Program (SBIR). A government program that supports research and development for small businesses across the United States.

Small Business Technology Transfer Program (STTR). A government program that supports research and development for small businesses in conjunction with a U.S. research facility.

Tell-Test Education. The system of education whereby a teacher lectures to students and tells them what they have to learn and then tests them on the material.

Transparency of Design. A game with transparency of design allows interested players to learn how the game simulation works and possibly modify the game itself.

"Twitch" Games. Games that force the player to react quickly to visual stimuli in order to continue playing.

Wargame. Those games that simulate battles or wars without engaging in actual combat.

Index

Gamedev.net

The most comprehensive game development resource

- ○ The latest news in game development
- ○ The most active forums and chatrooms anywhere, with insights and tips from experienced game developers
- ○ Links to thousands of additional game development resources
- ○ Thorough book and product reviews
- ○ Over 1,000 game development articles!
  Game design
  Graphics
  DirectX
  OpenGL
  AI
  Art
  Music
  Physics
  Source Code
  Sound
  Assembly
  And More!

Gamedev.net